C U R R E N C Y

D O U B L E D A Y

COLLECTION MANAGEMENT

10/06	0 ~ 1	
10-8-09	1 - 1	8/9/09
6/12	4 - 1	12/11

THE WEST POINT
WAY OF LEADERSHIP

THE
WEST POINT
WAY OF
LEADERSHIP

*From Learning Principled
Leadership to Practicing It*

COL.
LARRY R. DONNITHORNE
(RET.)

CURRENCY

DOUBLEDAY

NEW YORK / LONDON / TORONTO / SYDNEY / AUCKLAND

A CURRENCY BOOK

PUBLISHED BY DOUBLEDAY
a division of Bantam Doubleday Dell Publishing Group, Inc.
1540 Broadway, New York, New York 10036

CURRENCY and DOUBLEDAY
are trademarks of Doubleday,
a division of Bantam Doubleday Dell Publishing Group, Inc.

Book design by Terry Karydes

Library of Congress Cataloging-in-Publication Data

Donnithorne, Larry.
The West Point way of leadership: from learning principled
leadership to practicing it / Larry Donnithorne.
p.   cm.
Includes bibliographical references.
1. Leadership.   I. Title.
HD57.7.D66   1993   93-28912
658.4'092—dc20   CIP

ISBN 0-385-41703-9

First Edition

1 3 5 7 9 10 8 6 4 2

To my wife, Fran,
and our four children,
Mark, Jeff, Amy, and Rebekah

Contents

Contents

THE WEST POINT
WAY OF LEADERSHIP

WHITE
PHOSPHORUS!

1

The U.S. Military Academy at West Point takes the task of building leaders very seriously. Since its inception in 1802, the Academy has refined a unique system for teaching leadership. A consultant I know explained the Academy's uniqueness this way:

> At every Fortune 500 institution in America, people are taught ethics. At West Point, people are taught character.

"Leader of character" is the phrase the Academy uses to describe the kind of leader it wants its cadets to become. A leader of character has all of the qualities we normally associate with leaders—ambition, confidence, courage, intelligence, eloquence, responsibility, creativity, compassion—and one thing more which we unfortunately overlook too frequently among civilian leaders: A leader of character is absolutely trustworthy, even in times of great stress, and can be depended upon to put the needs of others—the organization, the community—above personal considerations—not now and then, or when the spirit moves him, or when it will look good on his résumé—but in every instance.

I've taught leadership at West Point. I also studied it as a cadet. The program has helped me understand what is expected of a leader and how to meet those expectations. It is that system that I will describe here. Parts of it may sound as exotic to outsiders as the *Book of Five Rings,* the manual for samurai warriors, once seemed to Westerners. For corporate leaders, extensive sets of rules and a strict hierarchy such as the Academy upholds may seem old-fashioned. But the leaders at West Point know something that may sound paradoxical: Rules—especially the rules of leadership—set the stage for initiative, loyalty, and teamwork of a highly powerful nature. Let me give you an example.

In 1966, while still a senior at West Point, I volunteered for Vietnam as my first tour of duty. I could have avoided the war for a time by choosing an assignment elsewhere. It was not an easy decision—I was already quite interested in my bride-to-be. But I found myself thinking, "I've spent four years learning leadership. Where can I practice it better than where the action is?" I was assigned to a platoon which was building roads on the coast north of Cam Ranh Bay.

Building roads is muddy work, which as a lieutenant in the Corps of Engineers I could have supervised at a distance, yet I made it a point to be out there with my soldiers all the time. As long as they were in the mud, I would be in the mud.

I also made it a point to learn how to operate all the various vehicles that my platoon used, many of which were unique to construction units. I did not seek out this knowledge for my personal edification. West Point had taught me the importance of appreciating what my troops could and could not do, so that I could set goals for them which would be challenging but feasible. The Academy had convinced me that it was as important for *the leader* to know the work of the subordinates as it was vital for the subordinates to know it themselves. It increased my troops' trust in my leadership to know that I knew what they knew.

One afternoon one of my soldiers was out cutting a rough road by bulldozer, and he got his vehicle stuck in a rice-paddy irrigation ditch. No matter how he tried, he couldn't get out. Night was approaching, and night was terribly dangerous—after dark, the threat of enemy attack was greatly increased.

That afternoon, when I arrived on the scene, most of my soldiers and two platoon sergeants were already there trying to help, but nothing seemed to work. I studied the situation for a long time, looking carefully at the predicament of the stuck bulldozer. I finally went to the driver and asked him to try using his blade to lift in one direction, to crank one track in a certain way, and then give power to the other track. He thought about my suggestion, gave it a try, and dramatically the bulldozer climbed up, up, up—and out of the ditch. We were able to return to our compound before nightfall.

A platoon sergeant approached me later and, with a grin, said, "White phosphorus!" I turned to him, puzzled.

"What?" I asked.

"White phosphorus—West Point!" he said. "I knew you could do it." In the Army, WP is an acronym standing for a white phosphorus artillery round. It's one of the most powerful explosives—it burns white hot and creates a fire that can't be smothered. For the sergeant, the acronym also stood for West Point.

The sergeant got it right. A West Point education is a powerful curriculum for meeting the demands of leadership. The system is as rigorous as it is thorough. It works on the body, the mind, and the heart. As leadership education, it can't be smothered.

The Academy is committed to giving cadets the experience and training to ensure that they develop "the right stuff." The moment you walk onto the campus along New York State's Hudson River, you enter a culture where nothing is valued more highly than sound leadership. From the statues of generals George Washington, Douglas MacArthur, Dwight D. Eisenhower, and George S. Patton, to the respect and attentiveness the cadets display toward one another, toward their superiors and the work they do, the importance of superb leadership is reinforced at every turn.

From the very first day, cadets find themselves submerged in a cauldron of experiences, which are frequently complex and fast-paced. At first, there isn't even enough time to think. But *every one of these experiences, every aspect of every day of the cadet's training, is designed to teach leadership.* West Point's goal is to take a group of select young men and women and, through this cauldron of experiences, imbue them with an enhanced capacity to lead others. Indeed, it may be difficult to find anywhere in the world a program which combines the elements of leadership development as comprehensively as West Point's. Many of these experiences and lessons are presented in the pages that follow. Some can be duplicated in the civilian world to achieve great benefits.

"GIVE ME ANYONE, ANYONE EXCEPT A SCHIZOPHRENIC, AND I'LL TURN HIM INTO A LEADER."

So said General Dave Palmer, a former Superintendent of West Point. The Academy has never believed that only a few human beings are endowed from birth with leadership's requisite traits, and others need not apply; this is demonstrably a myth, although a myth with considerable popular support. The often-heard phrase "leaders are born, not made" neglects the potent possibility that leaders are both. As organizational theorist H. A. Simon put it, "A good executive is born when someone with some natural endowment (intelligence, vigor and some capacity for interacting with his fellow men) by dint of practice, learning and experience, develops that endowment into a mature skill."*

Although the essence of leadership—influencing other people toward the achievement of shared goals—may sound deceptively simple, leadership as The Academy teaches it is practiced in the context of real life. Learning to lead is every bit as complex as learning to become a mature, productive adult all over again. At West Point we take this literally: We teach leadership by teaching the raw recruit how to do everything—from eating to walking to thinking—in a new way, a way that will build his or her new stature. That process, and

---

* As quoted by Kenneth and Miriam Clark, editors, in *Measures of Leadership* (West Orange, New Jersey: Leadership Library of America Inc., 1990), p. 547.

how it can be adapted to organizations outside the military, will become clear in the pages that follow.

The core of our program is more than strategy or vision: It's the philosophy and practice of a set of values. Standing in the mud with your people, learning their work, staying with their problems until solutions are found—these derive from the basic values of leadership taught at the Academy.

The values began with the organization. West Point, with a history almost as old as the nation itself, has been a foundry of leaders since its inception during Thomas Jefferson's presidency. Among the military leaders who have graduated from West Point are Ulysses S. Grant, Robert E. Lee, Douglas Mac-Arthur, Dwight D. Eisenhower, Omar Bradley, George Patton, Maxwell Taylor, Brent Scowcroft, and, more recently, Norman Schwarzkopf. West Point has also provided the United States with many leaders who proved their effectiveness in the civilian world—among them, Robert Wood, who turned Sears Roebuck into a household name; Rand Araskog, chairman of ITT; Wesley Posvar, former president of the University of Pittsburgh; and Frank Borman, former astronaut and former CEO of Eastern Airlines. West Point graduates have served as CEOs of dozens of major corporations (including Coca-Cola, General Dynamics, Sperry Corporation, and Du Pont Chemical), presidents of many colleges and universities (among them, Columbia University, Georgia Institute of Technology, and the University of California at Berkeley), and in every level of federal, state, and local governments. Leaders trained at West Point were in charge of building the Panama Canal and other public works and have played an important role in international diplomacy. Two of the first three men to land on the moon were West Pointers.

This long-term success in developing world leaders—both in the civilian and military orbits—suggests West Point's is a time-tested, integrated model for producing leaders. As a model, it offers numerous insights into the task of developing leaders, as well as in developing active leadership skills in oneself.

WHAT CIVILIAN LEADERS CAN LEARN FROM THE MILITARY

The differences that exist between military and civilian leadership are differences in degree, not in kind. In the armed services, one notices the emphasis on subordination—not only to the will of leaders, but frequently of an individual's desires and goals. A life in the military requires a healthy amount of stoicism; one inevitably makes personal sacrifices in the face of the good of larger entities—one's platoon, one's company, one's country. When your business is often life and death—as it is for the soldier in wartime—you learn to take your business seriously. You learn to pay constant attention to those around you, and to yourself. You learn to take nothing for granted. You can't afford to do any less. Because the stakes are as high as they can get, certain leadership behaviors are achieved at a more accelerated pace than might be the norm in most civilian organizations. Among these are a higher level of obedience, a more lasting sense of loyalty, and the qualities of attention, self-sacrifice, and honesty. But today, when organizations have to change on a dime, like a platoon facing unexpected enemy fire, these qualities and the ability to learn them quickly all count.

There is often a certain resistance in the civilian world to the idea that something worthwhile can be learned from the military. My guess is that, for those who have no firsthand contact with the service, their image of the prototypical officer comes from the opening of the movie *Patton*, in which George C. Scott, brilliantly depicting one of West Point's most famous graduates, backed by an enormous American flag, coarsely urges hundreds of soldiers to go out and make those other guys spill their guts for their country.

This is not the prototypical military style, and I would go one step further to state that there is no established military style of leadership at all. Illustrating this point, John Gardner, in his book *On Leadership*, pointed to the diversity of leadership styles of military commanders. He described George Marshall as a "self-effacing, low-keyed man with superb judgement and a limitless capacity to inspire trust." Douglas MacArthur was "a brilliant strategist, a farsighted administrator, and flamboyant to his fingertips." Dwight D. Eisenhower was "an outstanding administrator and coalition builder," George Patton "a slashing, intense combat commander," and Bernard Law Montgomery a gifted and temperamental leader of whom Churchill said, "In defeat, indomitable; in victory, insufferable."

The same claim can be made—and, indeed, has been— that there is no common "corporate leadership style." In *Leaders: The Strategies for Taking Charge*, Warren Bennis and Burt Nanus, drawing from their study of a large number of successful corporate CEOs, observed that "there seemed to be no obvious patterns for [the CEOs'] success. They were right-brained and left-brained, tall and short, fat and thin, articulate and inarticulate, assertive and retiring, dressed for success and dressed for failure, participative and autocratic. There were more variations than themes. Even their managerial styles were restlessly different."

I would argue that executive styles are not very important. The roots of sound leadership—be it civilian or military—are in ideals: moral principles (such as justice and beneficence), high-minded values (loyalty, integrity, consideration for others), and selfless service—all of which this book examines in practical detail. But these values hold no power unless they are practiced. The reader will see how to enact a self-disciplined leadership designed to go beyond personal ambition to serving the best interests of other people, to goals and commitments larger than oneself. It is precisely these larger-than-self commitments that give a leader the clearest sense of possibilities, the potential for his or her achievements.

THE FOUR PASSES OF LEADERSHIP

A very unsuspecting eighteen-year-old, I arrived at West Point in 1962, dressed in Bermuda shorts and a red shirt. I went to the gymnasium carrying a small, tan suitcase, signed all the appropriate papers, and headed for the quadrangle enclosed by the cadet barracks, called Central Area.

There I saw a uniformed cadet whom I could only describe as looking perfect. He wore a red sash, which, then as now, marks those cadets in charge of the first-day initiation. He saw me from a distance and called, "Hey, you in the red shirt! Post over here!"

I didn't yet have any familiarity with cadet or military terminology, but I guessed that "post over here" meant he wanted me to approach him. So I walked over and stuck out my hand. "Hi, I'm Larry Donnithorne," I said with a smile. I expected him to return the favor and say, "Hi, I'm Joe Smith, welcome to West Point."

He didn't. What he said—and this is almost an exact quote—was, "*Smackhead, do you think anyone around here cares what your first name is?*" Predictably, I was at a loss for words.

We went through a prolonged ceremony in which he commanded me to drop my suitcase. I leaned over and set it down. "*No, smackhead,*" he said. "*I said* drop *your bag!*" This time, I leaned over and let it drop the last two inches. We went through this process ad infinitum until I reached the point where I made no movement at all except to open my fingers and let the suitcase drop. This finally satisfied him.

Upperclass cadets don't treat the first-year cadets, known as plebes, this way any longer. Today, the prevalent style of leadership in the Army has been evolving to a less autocratic one, which gives greater weight and respect to subordinates than has been the primary mode in the past. At West Point, the obligation emphasized for the upperclass cadet is *to behave toward a plebe the way a leader should toward a subordinate.* On the first day, the young man or woman in the red sash speaks very firmly, in businesslike terms—but without the bag-dropping exercise. He or she tells the new cadets what they need to know, where they need to go, and what they are going to do. The upperclass cadet makes sure the new cadet understands, and if anything has been left unclear, he or she explains again.

The bag-dropping ritual did, however, embody one fundamental principle that remains unaffected by the changes in the cadet relationship: Before plebes can learn the skills of leadership, the Academy must first remind them of all they don't know.

In fact they know a great deal. They have been chosen for West Point because of what they know and are able to do. Indeed, it is upon this very promising foundation that the Academy wants to build. They are capable young men and women. Many have been leaders in their communities and families. But here they are not leaders. Not yet. Thus, what the new cadets do not yet know is the crux of the matter which must be emphasized to them. In their own minds, they must become a *tabula rasa*. They must "start from zero." Because from this point on, the only thing that's important is what they don't know.

Cadets don't know how to lead soldiers well. They don't know how to motivate or train or reward or discipline effectively. They don't even know how to march, salute, or wear the West Point uniforms. The Academy makes it clear to them that they don't know a lot. Starting from zero is not easy; it's at best confusing, most probably frightening. Point Zero for new cadets is followership. Cadets spend a year learning the lessons of followership: self-discipline, stress- and time management.

From there, the cadets embark on four passes of leadership training.

✻ The First Pass shows how the Academy forges the bonds that strengthen the organization. Essentially this is done by emphasizing teamwork and the satisfaction of absorbing an institution's value system, one perhaps higher than their own.

✻ The Second Pass helps the individual begin to find his or her own voice in the organization by emphasizing direct or face-to-face leadership—an experience akin to first-level management positions in the corporate world—and moral reasoning, the basis of honorable leadership.

✻ The Third Pass teaches the self-reliance and leadership skills necessary to lead people who lead others. This is called indirect leadership.

✻ The Fourth Pass, executive leadership, which in corporate life occurs at the upper echelons of management, shows the cadets how to act in their organization's long-term interest.

"Passes" has echoes for me of a few core experiences, *repeated* many times over the course of one's life, but each time differently and with a different result. Each time we are challenged by a practical leadership task, we are changed by it—*if* we are reflective about the experience. The next time we face that situation, we will be a different person from before. Thus we will handle the situation differently, learning *new* lessons. West Point's leaders-in-training similarly make several passes over the basic elements of leadership from values to behavior —each time from a different perspective, first from the perspective of the beginner, later progressing all the way to the leader who is responsible for an entire organization.

While the parallel between the four passes through cadet

leadership and corporate management is obvious, the relevance of other aspects of the training may not yet be as apparent. You may be saying to yourself, "Well, that's all well and good for West Point. But what has it got to do with me?"

I believe it has everything to do with you. West Point's proven methods of leadership development are not merely applicable to the civilian world; I believe they offer an important corrective to the world of organizations that has come to accept chaos as naturally as we accept the air we breathe. Chaos may be pervasive, but it needn't be accepted as inevitable. West Point's traditional understanding of the value of rules, the value of honor, the point of living by your word—all of these are fundamentals that bring stability in the midst of chaos, provide a shelter from the storm, and will surely benefit any leader in any business.

STARTING
FROM ZERO:

Tearing Down Before

Building Up

2

Followership Is Job One

E very leader is a follower. No one commands an organization without restraints. For every leader, no matter how "supreme," there is always a higher authority who must be answered. The Chairman of the Joint Chiefs of Staff is responsible to the Commander in Chief. In turn, the President of the United States must answer to the Congress and the American people. Even the CEO of a multinational corporation has to respond to the board, the stockholders, the customers. Their success depends in a large part on how well they have learned to follow.

Followers' jobs are at their essence to do as they are told. They are asked to surrender—for a time—their independence and devote themselves exclusively to practicing the values of the institution they have joined. Each person who comes to West Point learns where one's individual authority ends and the institution's begins. In learning followership one attains an intimate understanding of the ways and values of the organization one's labor sustains. For us, followership is a form of self-mastery, mastering of the ego. So much effort is put by business into championing individual performers rather than the institution that people often forget the needs of the company they serve. West Point wants its young cadets to savor what it means to be a part—even a small part—of a great institution. Followership is the first step toward that recognition. And followership demands a great effort, especially from those who cherish their individualism.

THE FIRST STEP ON THIS PATH IS GETTING TO ZERO

If followership is the beginning of leadership, the beginning of followership is getting to zero: realizing all that you don't know, and then opening yourself to the possibility of being remade into something more.

This is important because one is not born a leader—one is made by self-effort into a leader. In many tribes, initiation rites mark a young boy's transition from youth into adulthood. An adolescent is sent alone into the woods for several days and nights to confront his fear and ignorance—almost like a second birth. At West Point, we also insist that entering cadets—who are known as plebes—start from zero.

Most plebes enter the Academy cocksure and confident from the great successes they've already had in high school, so their direction is to evolve into self-absorbed, self-congratulatory, inconsequential leaders. To feel the full impact of the training West Point is about to give them, they must understand they are becoming a part of something much bigger than they are—an institution, with a set of rules and traditions, and a great mission for the country. These leaders-in-training need to know the extent of their own limitations before they can begin to grow further as leaders.

This understanding is gleaned through a hard lesson in subordination—one learned with great difficulty by plebes who are bright, confident, proud eighteen-year-olds, fresh from successful high school careers where they excelled both academically and athletically. But it is Job One.

On their first day on campus—Reception Day, known by cadets as R-Day—the Academy strips plebes of their most basic possessions: the identifying marks of their individuality. For the first few weeks they are nearly as anonymous and interchangeable as newborn babies.

R-Day is a meticulously organized event executed with clockwork precision by the upperclass cadets. The plebes—about thirteen hundred of them—begin to arrive on campus early in the morning. The first thing that is taken away from them is control over their own time. After a brief indoctrination, the plebes are hurried through a multitude of tasks at a pace so rapid that they literally do not have time to look around and see where they are or where they're going. Most West Point graduates describing R-Day use words like, "disorienting," "confusing," "chaotic." Dwight D. Eisenhower wrote about his first day at West Point: "I suppose that if any time had been provided to sit down and think for a moment, most of us . . . would have taken the next train out."

The men are shaven nearly bald, and women cadets' hair is shorn just below the ears. Off come the civilian clothes. All the plebes spend the first half of R-Day running urgently from one point to the next, wearing gray T-shirts, black shorts, knee-length black socks, and heavy black brogans. Putting them through their paces are upperclass cadets impeccably attired in tailored dress gray uniforms, and red sashes which mark them as R-Day instructors. The plebes' individual desires are replaced by their leaders' one group goal: to look as good as possible at the finale of their first day—the swearing-in ceremony on the Plain.

By the end of an eight-hour day they appear on the parade field reborn in full-cadet uniform, marching in formation before an audience of the parents and family who brought them only hours earlier.

The same day the Academy teaches cadets to march and to dress, it teaches them how to eat. At each meal during their first summer at West Point—known as Beast Barracks—they are required to sit at attention, buttocks resting on the front half of their chairs, with their backs straight and both feet flat on the floor. They are forbidden to look about freely; they must keep their eyes on the top rims of their plates. They can take only small bites of food and, after placing each bite in their mouths, must put their forks on their plates and their hands in their laps before beginning to chew. They may not talk with one another.

Their conduct is enforced by their squad leader, who sits at the head of the table in the position known as Table Commandant. This cadet frequently asks questions of the plebes which have prescribed answers that must be given to the letter. For instance, if the Table Commandant inquires, "How's the cow?" (slang for "How much milk is left?"), the plebe must reply, "Sir [or Ma'am], she walks, she talks, she's full of chalk! The lacteal fluid extracted from the female of the bovine species is highly prolific to the [nth] degree," (the "n" indicating the number of milk cartons on the table).

These rituals reinforce the intense concentration required to open the plebes' minds. Because they have to rethink the most basic aspects of their behavior, their character changes in response from one of self-limiting certainty to awareness, questioning, wondering. West Point is preparing them to change their lives. These rituals teach the basic skill necessary for the first phase of leadership development—self-mastery.

LEARNING THE RULES, AND THE VIRTUE OF FOLLOWING THEM

During Beast Barracks such a high volume of information must be absorbed, and so many tasks must be accomplished, that there is not even time to think. Plebes are kept so busy, and have so little time, that free choice is not even an option. They are simply learning what their business is, and how to follow its rules accurately and instantly.

The young cadets have heretofore not experienced the level of subordination to authority demanded at West Point, and many find their new environment disconcerting. But it is a carefully considered and constructive process, designed to encourage two seemingly paradoxical behaviors: obedience and initiative.

While demanding subordination and greatly curtailing individual choice, West Point also leaves the cadets just enough room to be inventive. The difference between West Point's system and ies of truly extreme subordination is that, in the latter, ative is not only discouraged, it is sometimes outlawed— for example, in the ex-Soviet bloc countries which used techniques of brainwashing, thought and information control. Subordination at the Academy is primarily a test, the successful result of which is the gain of self-command—and more and more independence—by the cadets.

Ultimately, the self-discipline that enables cadets to meet this challenge will serve them well. They will become the kinds of leaders who can postpone gratification in pursuit of a long-term goal.

LISTENING AT A GUT LEVEL

West Point believes there are clearly times when leaders have the responsibility to tell subordinates exactly what they are expected to accomplish, and subordinates have the responsibility to do exactly as they are told. Leaders want their plebes to concentrate utterly on what they hear. They want them fully focused on the job at hand, not daydreaming about what they're having for dinner or their friends back home or what they wish they were doing instead. They must focus on what they are being asked to do at that moment—and then they must act, swiftly, surely, decisively. What plebes must learn is to listen. Listen carefully and intensely, listen to every order at a gut level, as if their lives depended on it.

A long-standing West Point tradition gets the cadets into the habit of this level of listening: When a plebe is asked a question by an upperclass cadet or an officer, there are only four answers at his disposal. Any extraneous words immediately trigger the question, "Mister [or Miss], what are your four responses?" To that query, the only answer is "Sir [or Ma'am], my four responses are 'Yes, sir'; 'No, sir'; 'No excuse, sir'; and 'Sir, I do not understand.' " That is all they are allowed to say.

This system doesn't always seem fair to plebes. For example, if an upperclassman asks, "Mister, do you call that a polished belt buckle?" the plebe will naturally want to explain the extenuating circumstances that led to this lapse. The words form in his mind: "Sir, another plebe accidentally bumped into me on the way to formation." But he is restricted to the four answers and they must suffice. His only available answer is, "No, sir." If the upperclass cadet asks why, the only appropriate answer is, "No excuse, sir." The cadet learns to live with the injustice; life isn't always fair. He is learning that no matter what the circumstances, he is expected to live up to his obligations. At this early stage in his career, that may only mean presenting himself with proper military dress and bearing. Later, he will hold other lives in his hands.

MAKING A HABIT
OF SUCCESS

West Point does not teach cadets to listen merely for the good of their souls. It does so because a cadet's success depends on his understanding of the demands being placed on him. After all the briefings and all the practice and all the lecturing is over, the responsibility rests squarely on the cadet's shoulders. The Academy sends him out to do the job, fully expecting that he will accomplish *everything* he sets out to do. This is the key: The cadet is expected to succeed. There is "no excuse, sir," for a lesser performance.

Living by this philosophy leads to an impressive kind of persistence, as I learned as a young lieutenant during my first tour in Vietnam. One day my company commander sent me to battalion headquarters with a list of seven things to do. There were people to see, instructions to be acquired, and different supply items to be procured, including maps and acetate. (The latter was in extremely short supply.) I remember how determined I was at a subconscious level to accomplish all seven tasks, even though I wasn't sure how I would get the job done.

It wasn't easy. Predictably, the acetate was a problem. I had to do a lot of fast talking to convince a supply sergeant, who had only a small amount, to give me any. I kept plugging until eventually I either convinced him it was for a good cause or that the easiest way to get rid of me would be to hand over some acetate.

When I got back to my commander, he was quietly but visibly surprised as I checked off my list with every request fulfilled. He hadn't expected me to succeed totally, but the notion of failure never entered my mind. This is the West Point standard for excellent followership. There is no time to be wasted making excuses for not performing, no time to lose covering up your tracks. *There is only time to do the job—for success.*

This is the extension of the four answers: "No excuse, sir." West Point had trained me to understand that my superior officer only wanted results. He didn't want to hear any elaborate explanation of why I couldn't fulfill his orders. (It was also clear that he did not want me cutting corners either—especially moral ones.)

TEACH PEOPLE TO REWARD THEMSELVES

The best followers are self-motivated. They are secure in their ability to do a job. Their sense of purpose, and of self-worth comes from themselves, not from others. Leaders must avoid the trap of giving rewards too freely, because first, it demeans the value of the work done, and, second, it encourages followers to become *dependent* on rewards for successful performance. In their plebe year at West Point, cadets discover early on that they are rarely clapped on the back for a job well done. Hence, they learn a most important lesson of followership: the job well done is its own reward.

I realize that not giving out myriad rewards may sound at best stern and at worst cruel—especially when compared with trendy management texts that preach the gospel of rewarding employees with everything from raises and bonuses to gold stars and M&M's. Sometimes rewards are indeed a boost—but they should not become trivial. West Point saves them for only thoroughly important achievements.

However, the Academy encourages self-rewards, by deliberately setting up experiences wherein the plebe learns to find great internal satisfaction from performing work well. This means that he learns to work not just in spurts—for an "attaboy" or a pat on the back—but instead embodies a consistently high standard. You can meet this standard only if you become your own reward-giver.

When I was a plebe, for one infraction or another, my squad leader demanded that I memorize the words to "The Corps," a very long and complicated cadet song, by breakfast the following morning. That night, I stayed up with a flashlight under my blanket reading and memorizing. The next morning at breakfast, he stared me in the eyes and said, "Let's hear it." I proceeded with the lengthy recitation. When I finished, perhaps surprised at my performance, he said *absolutely nothing*. I'm not even sure that I memorized it perfectly, but if I made a mistake, he didn't find it.

The only reward he gave me was silence. I returned to my food knowing I had performed beyond his expectation. I was happy. My pleasure was truly sufficient reward. Eventually, cadets learn the intrinsic satisfaction of building their own internal standards, by which they come to know when they've done a job well.

Excellent performance should be the standard expected in the civilian world. There is "no excuse" for not performing. The best leadership enables people to work as independently as possible. Most subordinates would prefer a leader who leaves them alone, lets them do their jobs, and appreciates work that is done well.

Under these conditions, a simple acknowledgment of work well done can be worth more than time off or money. One West Point tactical officer would occasionally leave in a cadet room a paper plate on which he scribbled a positive word or two—"Good job!"—and his initials. Because these plates were unique and rare, they were prized by cadets.

When I was stationed in Korea with the Army engineer units, although it was peacetime, there was always tension in the demilitarized zone. North Koreans would occasionally tunnel under and start a firefight, and so we knew that combat was a real, though unlikely, possibility every day. Whenever I had a particularly good day, my commander would say, "Donnithorne, you struck a blow for freedom today." That was all the reward he offered; it was enough.

BUILDING IN EACH INDIVIDUAL A GROUP IDENTITY

Leaders of successful organizations make sure their followers are proud to be part of the company. For this to happen, the followers as individuals, and the organization as a whole, must have values in common.

West Point works hard to help the cadets take on the values of the group as their own.

The entire West Point experience is designed to foster group values. Among the principal methods is teaching the cadets their history—our history.

For example, plebes must learn military ranks, insignias, shoulder patches, and medals—and what they are awarded for. The memorization of these details requires intense concentration on the part of the plebe, but the benefit vis-à-vis group values is immediate. After these lessons, when cadets come in contact with any person in any branch of the military, they will see not only the individual before them, but exactly where that individual fits into the group.

Some of the material the cadets are asked to memorize may initially seem at best trivial and at worst harassment to them. For instance, they may be called upon to recite the number of lights ("Three hundred and forty lights, sir.") in Cullum Hall (one of the Academy's assembly halls); the number of gallons ("Seventy-eight million gallons, sir, when the water is flowing over the spillway.") in the Lusk reservoir (which provides West Point with water); and the Academy definition of leather:

> *If the fresh skin of an animal, clean and divested of all hair, fat and other extraneous matter, be immersed in a dilute solution of tannic acid, a chemical combination ensues; the gelatinous tissue of the skin is converted into a non-putrescible substance, impervious to and insoluble in water. This, sir, is leather.*

There are several important reasons why West Point requires the memorization of such information. Among them are:

✳ In the military—indeed in civilian organizations as well —there will be times when one must do what one has been told without hesitation (any crisis situation, for example). Reciting these details at the whim of an upperclassman teaches the cadets to be clearheaded under pressure.

✳ There is a lingering belief among even the most liberal observers at West Point that a little bit of "doing what you're told no matter what" does a follower a great deal of good.

✳ Learning this information by heart further entrenches the cadets in a shared culture and a camaraderie that binds them to one another.

✳ Perhaps the most important value of the memorization is maintaining a tradition that links today's cadets with cadets of the past. When it is stressed that generations of leaders-in-training—from Ulysses S. Grant to Dwight D. Eisenhower to Norman Schwarzkopf—have memorized the same passages and overcome the same obstacles, the cadets become bound not only to one another but to a tradition of leadership known as "the long gray line."

On the cadet's third day the central feature of this tradition is articulated at a lecture which is their first introduction to the honor code. A speech that Douglas MacArthur gave to West Point cadets in June of 1962, expressing the values which had animated his fifty-three-year career of military service, is heard:

> *You are the leaven which binds together the entire fabric of our national system of defense. From your ranks come the great captains who hold the nation's destiny in their hands the moment the war tocsin sounds. The Long Gray Line has never failed us. Were you to do so, a million ghosts in olive drab, in brown khaki, in blue and gray, would rise from their white crosses thundering those magic words—Duty—Honor—Country.*

Most organizations are all too happy to rewrite, ignore, or even abandon their history. Instead, West Point constantly evokes great leaders from the Academy's past to deepen the cadet's respect for the institution's traditions—and for his or her place in "the long gray line." This rhetoric has more practical uses as well. A cadet who is forcing himself to perform tasks that he doesn't want to do may well think: This doesn't make sense to me. But MacArthur did it before me. Grant did it. Patton did it. This must be part of what turned them into great leaders.

KNOW YOUR BUSINESS

The attitude—common in large American corporations—that a good leader can be effective in any industry should be anathema to all leaders. Leaders need to know the particulars of the jobs they are responsible for. This knowledge can save time, money, and sometimes lives.

When he lectured at West Point in 1987, General John Wickham, former Army chief of staff, recalled that, as a young lieutenant, a wizened old platoon sergeant took him out each night to teach him to operate every one of the weapons used by the company. That was how Wickham learned the jobs of each soldier he was leading. He came to know what his men were—and weren't—capable of and could therefore make better decisions concerning which missions were feasible. Knowing that his decisions were based on an accurate understanding of their abilities increased his men's confidence in him as well.

At West Point, cadets learn their business from the bottom up beginning with the tools they use. They learn what their M16 rifles, hand grenades, and bayonets are made of and how they are used. They learn to take them apart and put them together. Cadets develop relationships with their tools that are almost human. A soldier's life may depend on his rifle. It never leaves a soldier's hand. He sleeps with it by his side. Drills make them physically and psychologically comfortable with their weapons.

One dramatic drill brings the ultimate consequences of their work home to the cadets. Wielding a rifle with a long blade mounted on its tip, the plebes are asked loudly by a squad leader,

"What is the spirit of the bayonet?"

They reply, "To kill, sir!"

"What makes the grass grow?"

"Blood makes the grass grow, sir."

Soldiers must fight and leaders must make sure that lives are not lost in vain. "When we reached the Rhine in World War II," General Omar Bradley once said, "it was not necessary that I knew how to build a bridge, but it was very helpful that I knew what was involved so I could see that the bridge engineers received sufficient time and logistical backup." A solid grounding in the details of their business will only help leaders as their responsibilities increase. This is especially true, as we will see later, when a leader reaches the highest level and is charged with the responsibility of seeing the big picture and guiding the organization accordingly.

LEARNING TO LOVE THE DETAILS

Oliver Wendell Holmes wrote of "the great forces that are behind every detail." West Point believes in those great forces —and that is why mastering every detail, from the memorization of trivia, to the perfectly polished belt buckle, to the ins and outs of an M16 rifle, are so important.

The mastery of details is good practice for leaders—one that comes in handy when the stakes are high.

As General Dave Palmer, former Superintendent at West Point, told me, "the devil is in the details." He meant that the greatest of plans, developed by the brightest of minds, must still be executed by conceiving and taking care of myriad small details. And the success of the plan depends on taking care of those details. (If the leader fails to pay attention to those details, then "the devil," following Palmer's analogy, will have worked his evil.)

Mastering details teaches cadets that perfection can be as simple as getting a high-gloss on your shoes. And once you've mastered shining shoes, perfection in more important things seems as if it's within your grasp, and not the province of someone else. West Point tries to make striving for perfection as elemental as breathing.

A hallowed element of leadership training at the Academy is "plebe knowledge," an established and lengthy set of information that plebes must memorize. It includes not only how many lights there are in Cullum Hall, and how many gallons are in the Lusk reservoir, mentioned earlier, but also the changing patter of "the minutes" and "the days."

At one time or another every plebe must perform the "minute caller" duty—standing in the hallway under the clock announcing in a loud, clear voice:

"There are five minutes remaining before dinner formation! The uniform is 'as for class.' I say again, there are five minutes remaining . . ."

Any mistake or slip of the tongue by the minute-calling plebe will provoke further probing by the upperclass cadet, and probably lead to the dreaded words, "Let's have 'the days,' mister!" This order demands a recitation of the useful trivia for the day—the date, the name of the officer in charge, the important sporting events or current movie of the day. The finale of the recitation recounts the number of days remaining before important upcoming events, which culminate in the graduation of the senior class: "Sir, there are 215 and a butt days until graduation!" (A butt is the remaining portion of the current day.)

Cadets undergo daily inspections for shined shoes, polished brass belt buckles, correct posture, tight "dressoff" (that shirts are tucked in and held in place by trousers or skirt), and straight "gig line" (the vertical column formed by the shirt's front placket and trouser fly). All this trivia that some in business think is irrelevant is actually a potent tool of quality control.

One cadet I know remembers a day during Beast Barracks on which he was required to report to an upperclassman's room for inspection twelve times, running back and forth from his own room at intervals of a few minutes. Each time he returned to the squad leader, something else was wrong: His hair was not properly combed; his shoe had become scuffed; the back of his shirt had become partially untucked; he didn't exactly remember a particular piece of plebe knowledge.

It became a challenge to the plebe and his roommates to get him to the point where the upperclassman would consider his appearance faultless. They all pitched in to meet the challenge, preparing him each time he returned to his room. It became a game, the object of which for the three cadets was to make this plebe *perfect*.

When the plebe arrived at the squad leader's room for the exhausting twelfth time, the squad leader found a hair on the back of the plebe's shirt that had fallen out after combing. The upperclass cadet told the plebe, however, that this time he could finally go back to his room without returning for further inspection. The plebe had had his own fun, though:

He'd made the squad leader work harder and harder each time to find his imperfections.

Not only are cadets made to do *everything* asked of them, they must do everything well. If they don't, their leaders come down hard on them. "Good shoes," they might say, "but a rotten dressoff." If they are considered not to have tried hard enough, they are forced—as was the cadet above—to keep on trying.

Faced with more to do than they can do well, plebes begin to learn to sort their tasks by priority, and balance the inevitable trade-offs. As long as they stay focused on the minutiae of the task, they can cope with internal stress.

This too is part of learning their business. Under high-stress, fast-paced crisis situations, such as combat, a leader can never work at the level of perfection. But having learned something about perfection as a routine, not as a peak state, a leader must learn to quickly surmise what alternatives are available, to assess his priorities, and to make the most of the time available.

GRADUATING FROM SUBORDINATION TO SELF-CONFIDENCE

What benefit can be reaped from an itch you can't scratch? Standing motionless on the parade ground at the position of "attention," cadets learn that "military bearing" means bearing an itch. They simply have no choice but to suppress the urge to scratch. A military formation would look conspicuously shoddy if it were made up of soldiers glancing to and fro or scratching themselves.

Such exercise of self-control is not intended merely to make plebes suffer. Nor is this level of subordination an exercise in systematic humiliation. Plebe year is training in accepting authority, but it is not demoralizing. Rather, as cadets reach the difficult goals set for them, their self-confidence and self-esteem increase—not to mention their self-command.

EXTRINSIC REWARDS

Earlier, I explained that West Point doesn't hand out rewards to cadets like candy at a birthday party. The Academy does, however, reward them—albeit infrequently—but only when a reward will *positively reinforce within followers the behaviors that leaders need from them.*

In selecting rewards, leaders should ask themselves, "What is this employee working for? What does she need most from this company?" A laborer may be working only to satisfy maintenance needs, and at this level, the valued rewards are monetary. Those in higher-level positions may be working instead to meet their needs for satisfying relationships or for creativity and personal growth. The individual's needs and desires should be carefully considered before rewards are distributed.

Although plebes may experience few extrinsic rewards at West Point, their first year, as it progresses, certainly becomes less punishing, bit by bit. For instance, those strict rules of the dining hall begin to slacken after the six weeks of Beast Barracks. While no radios are allowed in the plebes' rooms for their first six months, they are permitted afterward. After a while, when the plebes have learned their roles better, the upperclass cadets leave them alone most of the time.

However, their ultimate reward comes later in plebe year with the Recognition Ceremony. Throughout nearly the entire year, the upperclass cadets have treated the plebes with professional distance, addressing them as "mister" (or "miss"), and being addressed as "sir" (or "ma'am"). After a year of this behavior, the upperclass cadets—some hated, some feared, some admired and respected—shake hands with the plebes, welcome them to the upper class, and ask them their first names. Most cadets remember this moment—in which they are at last recognized and accepted as peers by the very people they have been emulating and performing for—as extraordinarily meaningful. Since the day they entered West Point the plebes have fought for this reward: the respect and acceptance of their peers.

At West Point, subordination is not harassment but a purposefully designed exercise in personal development. With skill, commitment, and willpower, plebes prevail and ultimately are admitted to the group.

3

Finding Courage in Fear

Fear is not a bad teacher. Fear strips one of pretensions and flattens false bravado. Fear brings a person face to face with the best and the worst of who he really is. To confront this bedrock of the self as part of the deepening experience of bringing the cadet to zero, the West Point program in physical education strips the cadet's self-image as thoroughly as R-Day strips them of all civilian trappings— clothes, hair, time. In its place, West Point uses the physical development program to teach leaders-to-be to develop real —not fake or adrenaline-high—levels of courage and perseverance. It does not teach courage *per se*, but rather the ability to manage fear so that a leader can take charge in a crisis.

I didn't realize how much I had gained from this training until I went to Vietnam.

I was a first lieutenant company commander, a veteran of all of seven months in Vietnam. My company had recently moved into a remote location in the central highlands. Late in the afternoon, while carrying my dinner to my tent, an incoming mortar round exploded about thirty feet ahead of me. It tore into one of my platoon leaders, a second lieutenant, who had been walking in front of me. "Larry," he screamed, "I'm hit!" I ran over to him. There was blood all over his body. More mortar rounds landed immediately. We were in the midst of a full-scale ground attack.

I ran into my tent and grabbed the radio microphone. Lying face down on the ground with the microphone in my hand, I remember thinking to myself, *"I'm scared out of my wits!"* I was twenty-two years old. No one had ever tried to kill me before. Now I was confronted by about two hundred Vietcong hoping to do just that. Scared as I was, something else in me took over, some resolute clearheadedness that I didn't know I had. Although in those moments I experienced fear more intensely than ever before in my life, I had to function through it—to "manage" it.

Despite the enormous tension, I was still in control and functioning. I called in artillery support, got the NCOs to mobilize our soldiers to fight off the attack, and called for a Medevac helicopter to evacuate the wounded, among them my platoon leader, who survived.

A ground attack is not one of the threats that civilian leaders usually encounter in their daily lives. But there are definite analogues between my experience and the dangers that civilian leaders face in corporate life. I contend that the act of learning to manage physical risk is a useful precursor to managing corporate danger.

At West Point I learned how to confront danger. All cadets are obliged to participate in physically risky sports—men take boxing and wrestling, and both men and women study gymnastics, survival swimming, and "combatives," a hand-to-hand system of self-defense. In addition, in order to graduate all cadets must engage in competitive sports and, for at least one season, participate in a team sport involving body contact and, hence, the danger of injury and pain. These requirements are important, not simply to toughen up the bodies of young soldiers, but to teach another essential leadership skill: acting courageously in the face of danger—managing one's fear.

✻ *Every leader faces risks.* The higher the risk, the more likely the leader's emotions will escalate to the point of fear. The best way to train yourself to manage fear when the stakes are high is to practice overcoming fear under controlled circumstances.

✻ *Every leader needs to be aggressive.* But a leader of character knows how to control aggressiveness and doesn't explode from lack of self-control.

✻ *Every leader needs to be completely devoted to bringing his organization to victory.* Aggressiveness is one of the characteristics which comes into play when the goal is victory. Yet every leader of character, civilian or military, understands that winning must be accomplished according to an established set of rules.

CONTROLLING AGGRESSIVENESS AND MANAGING FEAR: OVERMASTERY

Business leaders value aggressiveness, but unless they learn to handle the stronger emotions—fear and fury—aggressiveness will govern them rather than the other way around.

For some cadets the most difficult test is finding the courage to climb into the boxing ring and strike—hard—a classmate. For others, the epiphany comes when they realize that after the final bell rings and the match ends, they can walk away. Their aggressiveness need not carry over; it can be controlled.

I'm not suggesting that civilian leaders challenge one another and subordinates to a brawl. I am suggesting that leaders find a way to practice overcoming fear and make room in their organizations for courage to flourish. The German poet Rainer Maria Rilke believed in the value of "following your fear"—not quieting it or resolving it but experiencing it fully the way combatants do.

The greatest tool for keeping control in threatening situations is intense, repetitive training, a thorough rote grounding in boxing techniques. Cadets learn to throw a jab, a hook, and an uppercut; they shadow box and practice on body bags. The correct movements, such as shifting the hips while throwing a punch, are repeated so diligently that for many cadets they become second nature. Ideally, the cadet becomes so focused on his task and its techniques that his fear is subdued. He relies on what he knows, not what he's feeling.

This overmastery isn't as easy as it sounds. Boxing causes more anxiety in the cadets than any other aspect of their physical training. Many cadets—like many civilians—have never taken a punch in the nose. Suddenly they come face to face with their fear. As far as the cadets are concerned, the second worst thing that can happen to them is losing the match. But far and away the worst is that they may turn and run out of the ring. If they do, they must return, or they will not graduate. They must learn to face fear, understand it, and get a handle on how they react to its pressures. Only then can they be sure fear won't paralyze them at exactly the moment when they need to act calmly and knowledgeably.

Most cadets must struggle to bring themselves to strike a classmate—let alone strike hard. But a few cadets have the opposite problem—they are overeager to fight. In cadet lore these people are branded "headhunters." They must either learn to control their aggression or, in extreme cases, face expulsion from the Academy.

Two principles guide the cadets in their struggle:

✴ *Strike as hard as you can*—after all, the goal is victory. (Indeed, the accepted wisdom among most cadets is that drawing blood will enhance their grades.) If you pull punches, you won't win.

✴ *When a fight is over, it's over.* You shake hands with your opponent and walk away. You do not carry a fight's emotional baggage out of the ring.

There is, of course, a direct corporate equivalent to the lessons learned in boxing. It is precisely in the situations of greatest confusion, chaos, and corporate peril—for example, hostile takeovers or missed deadlines—that leaders must keep their heads, remember the fundamentals, and focus with cool concentration on exactly what must be done. Leaders in business, as in all fields, must be able to control their aggressiveness and manage their fears.

LEARNING TO WIN BY THE RULES

"There is no substitute for victory," Douglas MacArthur said. Yet leaders have a responsibility not only to win, but to win by the rules. We must put everything we have toward this goal—but we must also do it responsibly. Leaders of character bear a double responsibility: *how* they win is as important as *that* they win.

How do we learn this? One way is through competitive sports, each of which have a specific set of rules. MacArthur saw a direct relationship between team athletics and successful leadership. Serving on European battlefields during World War I, he became "convinced that the men who had taken part in organized sports made the best soldiers."

They were the most dependable, hardy, courageous officers I had. Men who had contended physically against other human beings under the rules of a game were the readiest to accept and enforce discipline.

Team sports also encourage an esprit de corps among companies consisting of cadets of all four classes. It is one of the few moments in cadet life when the rigid hierarchical structure is temporarily relaxed. When a plebe and a senior cadet play together on a football team, they are not the uppermost and lowest emblems on a totem pole, but two equals.

Playing a team sport is also one of the few opportunities for a plebe to excel individually. If a plebe cadet performs particularly well during a sporting event, he is celebrated by the entire company at the end of the game.

MASTERING FEAR BY RELINQUISHING CONTROL

To teach the art of managing fear and anxiety, the Academy draws from the emerging field of sports psychology. This began when one of the faculty, a trained psychologist, began to work with the football coach to assist athletes in managing their emotions on the day of a game, using psychological techniques. The parallels between the stress of competitive sports and the stress of other forms of competition—such as armed combat—made their success with football players at the Academy a matter of wider interest than simply enhancing football prowess.

Six primary techniques are used to help manage fear:

✳ *Visualization.* Creating and repeating a mental picture of the successful fulfillment of the desired performance (a run-off tackle, or a perfectly delivered sales pitch), as well as its outcome (ten yards gained, the sale clinched).

✳ *Self-regulating one's response to stress.* One is hooked up to stress-level and heart-rate machines while being shown film of the activity that is giving one particular trouble. If, for example, a cadet has difficulty climbing ropes, she can experiment with various personal responses while seeing the image of climbing rope over and over—until she finds the internal code which enables her to respond without stressing out. The heart-rate machine tells her when she is controlling her response successfully, and when she is not. This biofeedback approach can aid in one's learning to control the body's reactions to stress.

✳ *Establishing performance goals.* Establishing and maintaining measurable goals that will more easily enable one to make progress, bit by bit. This strategy prevents becoming adrift and confused over what one is striving for. An intercollegiate wrestler may strive, at first, to learn one new takedown per week. After a month, his next goal might be to win the starter slot. After accomplishing this, he might strive to win 80 percent of his varsity matches. If he had begun with this last goal, he would have been more likely to fail than if he had worked up to it step by step.

✳ *Focusing one's attention on appropriate cues during a performance to block out distractions.* In a football game, a defensive linebacker's goal is to move to the ball carrier and tackle him. But the movement by other players distracts him from knowing exactly where the ball is. By studying plays over and over, he learns to block out these distractions and practice concentration on the critical cues to his performance. This can be instructive for corporate leaders when contemplating their goals. There are always a thousand details competing for a leader's attention; but at any given moment only a few of them are in fact critical for his successful execution of his role as leader.

✴ *Maintaining a positive self-image and working from a position of possibility.* This is the David and Goliath syndrome. The player who looks into himself, and sees that he has good skills and believes he is well prepared (despite the obstacles), is much more likely to succeed than the player who has decided in advance that he will be defeated because the other player is stronger. Individuals with high self-confidence can form teams with likewise high confidence. A team—or a company—that believes it can win will not back down or be easily discouraged. Disciplined honing of skills and canny analysis of the weaknesses of one's opponents are the two ingredients to the recipe for beating the competition.

✴ *Attain overmastery and then relax. You'll know what to do.* Perhaps the toughest technique to learn is giving up conscious control and just letting yourself do all the things you've practiced and trained for so assiduously. One of the most fearful elements in the survival-swimming course is an exercise in which the cadets have to jump from a thirty-foot tower, fully clothed and carrying packs and rifles, into a swimming pool, where they take off their packs, their boots, and their shirts, which they tie into a temporary float. Of course, they practice every move several times beforehand. They know exactly what to do, but still, when the moment comes, most cadets hesitate, walk to the end of the diving board, pause, and finally plunge ahead. The elation of making the jump is enormous. They learn to let go of the false sense that they can control all circumstances. They learn that action breeds its own confidence. They win a small but important victory over themselves.

The Academy is not wise enough to show all cadets how to overcome or master their fears. One young cadet worked for over a year and a half, using the techniques mentioned above, trying to get over her fear of jumping from a height. None of the techniques worked. She was eventually eliminated from the Academy—for not being able to take that one single step off the tower. West Point would have done her no favor to overlook this. If she couldn't master her fear, it would have been risky to put her in a future situation where fear could take control of her best instincts. Unless you face your fear, it will be a constant and limiting partner.

FIRST PASS:

*Forging the Bonds that
Hold the Organization Together*

4

Honor Is the Language We Speak

The cadet's moral education, as with many other aspects of the Academy's program of leadership, begins with rules—with the honor code. When they enter, these budding leaders receive as their first and most important matter of business this law, which is short, sweet, and to the point: *"A cadet will not lie, cheat or steal, nor tolerate those who do."* The language of honor is spoken in this code.

Businesses are beholden to many laws, but none that are as deeply personal as West Point's. Maybe they should establish a simple code of their own. It is the bedrock lesson of every other leadership lesson the Academy teaches. Integrity of the kind mandated by the honor code is good for people—and good for business. It is profitable on at least two levels. In practical terms, a business that treats its customers, employees, and stockholders fairly will be able to build on its goodwill and prosper. But there is an even more important reason.

The honor code may seem simple, but it is the linchpin of a value system shared by all Army officers. West Point believes that an organization—like an individual—can fulfill its highest function only when guided by moral principles. Creating this particular sort of high-performance organization, in which every member is guided by the same bedrock principles, is not easy.

The Academy begins by taking the code very seriously. It introduces it, soon after cadets arrive, in a ceremony, not in a policy manual or a casual here's-how-we-do-business conversation. When the code is presented, the cadets are told that violating it will probably result in expulsion. Nothing less. At first, this is the sole reason that most plebes heed the code. When I learned what the punishments for lying, cheating, and stealing were at West Point, I decided that I had better stick to the truth because any punishment I might get for telling the truth would be less severe than getting thrown out of the Academy. I admit my level of moral reasoning was still quite limited at that age.

That is the first of three levels of moral growth that cadets experience, stages which roughly parallel those outlined by Lawrence Kohlberg in his book *The Psychology of Moral Development*. These three stages take the cadets from simply obeying a moral rule for reasons of self-interest to something much more vital in a leader of character—*the ability and will to make a moral decision springing from her deepest personal values and conscience*. There are no magic rituals that propel the cadets from one stage to another; but West Point does its best to expose them to enlightening incidents and provocative class discussions.

At the first stage—the self-serving stage—one obeys the

code for survival; if you don't, you're out. Eventually, though, it may occur to a cadet that he actually prefers living within a group whose members follow the code. It is more *pleasant*, more human, to be able to trust people. In this second stage— the social contract stage—people follow a moral precept because they are pleased with the resulting increase in collective prosperity, not simply to avoid punishment.

Still later comes the autonomous stage. One gradually comes to believe through the force of independent intellect that a life lived without moral guidelines is not worth living. This may not even occur until after graduation—indeed, some may never reach this stage of independent moral reasoning at all. But as people grow from youth to adulthood, they are more likely to successfully learn this moral reasoning and autonomy *later* in their development if, *early* in their development, they have learned moral principles and rules, and acquired the will to adhere to them.

BECOME YOUR WORD

Once the code has been introduced, the Academy teaches cadets how to become their word; how to live as if everything they say is as important as everything they do—because it is! To learn to be true to your word is almost like learning a foreign language. Most of us learn how to "color the truth" or evade it. The poet Byron said that we lie more to ourselves than to anyone else. So these earliest lessons in leadership are based on language. The reason this is so important is that words are the medium of action for any leader. Promises must be fulfilled. Requests must be acted upon. Empty words cause failed actions. We must live by what we say.

A series of honor classes illustrate how to live honorably —in keeping with the code—in situations taken directly from cadet life. They start with truth-telling at its simplest. Cadets may not lie—but they distinguish between lying and error, based on intent.

For example, a plebe, walking in the hall, is caught unawares by an upperclass cadet who booms, "Mister, did you shave this morning?" Startled, yet knowing an immediate reply is expected, the image of his lather-swathed face flashes before his eyes, and he answers, "Yes, sir!"

The image that crossed his mind is actually of the day before; at eighteen, he doesn't even need to shave every day. However, because he made a mistake, without the intention to deceive, he has not lied. Despite the fact that he hasn't violated the honor code *per se*, upperclass cadets and officers will encourage plebes to come forward and admit such errors anyway—but only under the general obligation of a civilized person to correct an error he has made.

Why put such emphasis on such an inconsequential untruth—particularly when there was no intent to deceive? Because if the plebe doesn't have to face the consequences of his mistake, it will be easier for him, on future occasions, to *intentionally* misstate—lie—and rationalize it as hardly different.

The next example is more clear-cut. A cadet who intentionally continues writing on a test after the instructor has given the command to "cease work" has indeed violated the code—this is considered cheating at the Academy. This behavior—dropping one's pen upon the command—becomes instinctive to cadets and so, assuming he heard the command, he is obligated to come forward and admit what he did. Other cadets who have seen the cadet continue writing are obligated to report him. Whether or not the cadet will be punished is determined later.

I repeat: West Point recognizes the importance of intent. There is a difference between acts that are intentional or deliberate, and those that are unintentional. This is the difference between a lie and a mistake. Dismissal for unintentional acts would be unusually harsh and indeed would make no sense—leaving no room for improvement, or for rectifying mistakes. However, one must be completely accountable for one's acts, whether lies or mistakes, though the former are far more grievous precisely because they are intentional.

Take "cadet borrowing." At West Point, cadets' doors are not locked. Therefore, a cadet who needs something—say, a book—can choose simply to take it from another cadet who is not in his room. The minimal protocol is that the borrower should write the other cadet a note explaining where the book is. However, sometimes, due to time pressure, cadets grab items without leaving notes. So long as the cadet honestly intended to return the item, his action is considered a serious error in judgment, but not stealing—therefore not an honor violation. But, if it is reported, it is a delinquency, and the cadet will be subject to demerits and punishment.

The Academy, of course, reserves the toughest condemnation for honor violations. An honor hearing is rather like a trial, at which evidence of the supposed violation, and its defense, is presented. Ultimately, the honor board will decide the verdict. If found guilty, the offending cadet is subject to dismissal from the Academy. (The only one who can save him from this fate is the Superintendent, who has the power to retain a violator under mitigating circumstances.)

I remember one cadet who was tried for two alleged honor violations at once. He was accused of copying another cadet's computer program from the cadet's hard disk. He merely changed the name and a couple of details, but then turned it in, stating it was his own work. He was found guilty—of cheating (which his plagiarism constituted) and lying—and was expelled from the Academy.

HOW HONOR BUILDS SHARED VALUES

The majority of the cadets say they have no trouble learning to observe the first three tenets of the honor code—living a life without lying, stealing, or cheating. But the fourth tenet —*not tolerating those who do*—presents them with a moral conflict.

Many have grown up with the principle that you don't "rat" on your friends. To an extent, West Point training reinforces that idea. The cadets learn to do everything possible to get each other through difficulties, just as the Army expects a commander to look out for every one of her soldiers. But the Academy also insists that each cadet obey the honor code. And this means that cadets may face the difficult situation of having to put the values of the institution ahead of a personal and strongly felt bond.

If West Point did not demand this last tenet, it could not build a high-performance organization. The danger of strong teams is that identification with the team can become stronger than the identification with the larger organization itself. The organization becomes "them" instead of "us." At West Point, the importance of the honor code's fourth tenet is to insist that, in the final analysis, the shared values of the organization are a more important bond than loyalty to one's peers.

Strong organizations, such as West Point, draw their strength from deeply rooted values, which are meant to unify individuals into a community. Leadership that is a cult of the self—charismatic leadership, for instance—can never be as strong as leadership rooted in the strength of shared values. Therefore, when a colleague violates the rules of honor, he is undermining the foundation and purpose of the organization —as well as every individual member of the organization. If West Point were to permit cadets to tolerate lying, rather than enforce the code, it would be elevating toleration as their highest value. Instead, the Academy teaches that there are acts we should not tolerate.

Ultimately, the lessons of honor teach the cadets to bond not only with their colleagues, but, even more strongly, with the values of honorable organizations. Identification with something larger than oneself helps an individual keep the common good in sight. The cadet keeps broadening himself, reassessing his individuality, then his role as part of the team, and then as part of the organization. His loyalty is not only to his own skill, or his own platoon—but to the Academy, and the values it represents, such as honesty, truthfulness, and respect for persons and property. One could call this double loyalty.

CHOOSING GOALS THAT
BREED ''DOUBLE LOYALTY''

A leader can foster double loyalty—to a team *and* to an organization—by inspiring in subordinates the sense that *they* are the organization. That the company is not "it" but "us." The leader can do this through language—by specifically referring to the organization as "us," because indeed it is the employees who make the organization. But most effective is leading the organization to serving goals which are broadly responsible, those which employees can feel right about promoting—in terms of the contribution they make to society rather than private gain.

If a leader redirects the total energies of an automobile company toward producing safe, reliable, economical, and ecologically sound cars, employees are more likely to feel positive about and committed to the organization, than if the goal is perceived to be nothing more than creating returns for stockholders.

In my capacity as president of the College of the Albemarle in Elizabeth City, North Carolina, I was recently presented with an alleged problem by my staff. A nearby college, in an attempt to diversify its historically black student body, began a scholarship program that attracted many of the best Caucasian students in the region—students who might have otherwise attended our college.

My staff saw this as a threat to our own liberal arts program. But I reassured them that we wanted to support, not hinder, the goals of the other college, because their goals served the greater social need of the region. I reasoned that we could shift our programs into other areas which would complement that other college's efforts, and still keep our faculty employed.

We had to put our institution's highest goals—to serve all the people of this region of North Carolina—above our own college's self-interest. The social needs of the whole region must be promoted, even if that would appear in the short term to "hurt" our college. But because our college should exist to serve the social good, it is my responsibility as its leader to see my obligations in those broad terms—and not in narrow terms which are organizationally, or personally, self-serving. The harder right here means not giving in to expediency. It means living out what West Point's program of moral education taught me: that survival and profitability are not ends. They are only means to the end of serving the public good. Leaders of character serve the public good, and go beyond not only their personal horizons, but even past the horizons of their colleagues, to serve everyone whose interests are affected. Identifying this larger goal for my staff made them proud to serve the larger purpose.

I was in my second year as a cadet when it dawned on me that the honor code made West Point the kind of organization I was proud to be a part of.

One night, after taps, I was lying in bed. The cadet subdivision inspector was making his rounds checking to see that all cadets who were supposed to be in their rooms were there.

In our barracks there were four rooms per floor. The cadet inspector merely stopped at each floor and called out, "All right?" and waited to hear the appropriate voice from each of the four rooms answering, "All right." He neither opened nor knocked on each door.

It dawned on me that he wasn't doing this out of laziness or expediency, but because he could trust us. We were cadets, we followed the honor code, and, therefore, would not lie about anything so elemental as room regulations. It occurred to me that this was a far superior system than having to check every tiny detail for lack of a serviceable and shared moral code.

This brief moment represented a giant step for me. In that instant, I had the profound realization that when individuals agree to behave with a prescribed set of high values they can have a much finer life than if they merely follow orders only because they have to, always looking for what they can get away with. This giant step was toward the autonomous adoption of those high values, and internalizing the concept of the harder right.

West Point cannot force this realization. Cadets have to reach it of their own accord; indeed, some never do. But the Academy does everything it can to help them get there.

5

"The Harder Right"

T he Academy teaches that a life directed by moral
guidelines promises deeper, richer satisfactions than
a self-serving, self-absorbed life. Many people, in as-
serting their justifications for immoral actions, claim they see
no payoff from moral behavior. They are like Scrooge brag-
ging about not having to buy Christmas presents because he
has no friends.

Cadets are expected to behave morally—not to mention
professionally—in all instances. Most people agree that leaders should always do the right—as opposed to the expedient
or the pragmatic or the popular—thing. West Point asks cadets to do this, and then to go one step further and reach for
what we call "the harder right."

Before a leader makes a decision, she must imagine her
range of influence as a circle. "The harder right" is usually the
decision that most positively affects the widest possible circle

of people. This requires a type of moral math that isn't instinctual—it must be practiced. Our instincts tell us to do right by those immediately around us—our friends, family, and immediate colleagues. But at West Point we urge that our leaders draw the circle ever wider, and take into consideration not just those nearest to them, but those in the Army, the community, the nation, the world. It takes years—and considerable devotion—to do this. It is a continual process of raising one's sights to include more and more.

At West Point this process begins with the careful cultivation of two capacities: the ability to discern, through moral reasoning and individual values, what the right thing is; and the strength of will to do it. As you will see in detail in the following chapters, each leadership pass requires the cadets to raise their moral sights a notch higher.

Two examples of the harder right, closely related in time, come to mind. Stationed in the town of Bao Loc, in the central highlands of Vietnam, as company commander in charge of one hundred and fifty U.S. Army Engineer soldiers, I was under extreme pressure to get an airfield built quickly in a remote province. So was my boss, Lieutenant Colonel Jim Lammie. One day, he flew in by helicopter to inspect our work, and expressed in no uncertain terms his objection to the manner in which we were placing the perforated-steel planks that were the foundation of the airfield.

He roared, "Who in the hell gave the order to do that?"

Immediately I said, "Sir, I did."

At West Point I had learned the habit of answering directly and honestly no matter what the consequences. In this instance, I acted on that habit again, despite the fact that I dearly wished the answer could have shown my own questionable judgment in a more favorable light. Lammie was angry, but this passed fairly quickly and we were able to get down to the serious business of rectifying my mistake. I could have done many things—blamed others, tried to reiterate my point of view with a different shading—but because of my training, I chose the harder right, the best decision for the most people, although it meant paying the price of a bruised ego.

A few weeks later another situation arose that concerned a young soldier whom everyone called Presley. One day, Colonel Lammie ordered me to suspend all operations and load up my men and equipment without delay. We were to move to a site thirty miles away where a bridge had been blown up by the Vietcong. Our assignment was to replace it with a portable bridge, thus quickly restoring the flow of food from the highlands to the lowland markets of Saigon.

However, we were nearing the end of the monsoon season, and unfortunately the brake pads on many of our vehicles had been worn away by the red-clay mud in which they had operated throughout the wet winter. For the time being, repair parts were unavailable.

Just prior to leaving, Presley, who drove the tractor-trailer on which we transported the bulldozer, came to me with a problem. "Sir," he said, "you know that I don't have any brakes on my tractor." He and I both looked at each other for a long moment. It was obvious to us that it was unsafe to drive any motor vehicle without brakes, but unthinkable to tow a forty-ton bulldozer on a tractor-trailer with no brakes. Finally, I said, "Presley, there's no use at all in our going if we don't take the dozer. We need the dozer's winch to move the damaged bridge." After another pause, I asked, "What can we do?"

He said slowly, "Well, sir, I guess I could try to drive it and use the engine to slow myself down on the hills, but, sir, that would probably blow the engine completely." I considered this very carefully and asked, "Presley, do you think you can do it?" I knew I was asking Presley to risk his life, and I was prepared in that moment for him to say no. I would have accepted this answer and scrambled for another solution— although to this day I don't know what I could have come up with. With a tremble in his voice, Presley said, "I'll try, sir."

As our convoy departed, Presley and I held our breaths— and pretty much kept them that way the whole thirty miles. By the time we arrived, Presley's engine was indeed destroyed —but he got there safe and sound, with the dozer in perfect condition. When he got out of the tractor he was an emotional wreck. Never before or since have I asked or received so much from a subordinate—or been as proud of one.

It was not easy for me to ask that much of Presley. He and I had been through combat together, and combat bonds soldiers strongly. He had become something like a brother or a son to me. My situation encompassed one of life's imponderables—how could I ask anyone, let alone a friend, to risk his life just to repair a bridge?

I believed then, and still do now, that it *was* the right thing. His making it through alive did not validate the morality of my decision. But in reality instead of theory, I am awfully glad I did not have to live with his death due to my decision. If he had died, I might have had many misgivings about my decision to have him drive that truck. Perhaps I would have eventually come to reason that I had done the right thing, even if he had been killed. If it was the right thing to do at all, it was right to have asked—whether he succeeded or failed.

In a sense, that was a test of my character. But a far greater measure of character was displayed by Presley, who chose the harder right and succeeded.

HOW TO CHOOSE THE HARDER RIGHT

There is no easy formula for making a moral decision in a split second, under great pressure, in a life-or-death situation, as Presley and I had to that afternoon in provincial Vietnam. Indeed, one learns to choose the harder right only after years of study and self-scrutiny. At West Point, we learn to slow the process to a crawl, and in our minds subject events to a great deal of questioning. Not analysis/paralysis, not scenario playing, but questioning designed to reveal what needs to be sacrificed so the greatest number of people can benefit. Indeed, if one has any doubts about a moral decision, here is a step-by-step series of questions that will sharply increase a leader's ability to reach for the harder right:

1. *What are the relevant facts of the situation?* First, a leader must clearly assess the situation at hand. What is the decision that has to be made? Who and what are involved, and how much is at stake? In the instance I've just recounted, the livelihood and well-being of a small region was temporarily stymied because its bridge had been destroyed by the Vietcong. Hundreds of trucks loaded with food were backed up.

Farmers were depending on the truckers to distribute the food they had grown and raised. Villagers for hundreds of miles around depended on them for their nourishment.

2. *What are the alternative actions available?* Honorable leaders don't make decisions solely on impulse. Even if there's only a moment to ponder, a leader should, as definitively as possible, balance the different choices available. At the time, I could see only two: either try to forge ahead and repair the bridge, although it meant risking Presley's life; or wait as the situation deteriorated at the bridge, causing more and more people to suffer increasing pain.

3. *Who will be affected?* An honorable leader tries to make the decision that will be most advantageous for the largest number of people. Not attempting to repair the bridge wouldn't have helped anyone—except Presley. On the other hand, by sending Presley on his perilous ride, I was enabling the rest of my company to do their jobs, and thus to help thousands of people in the region.

4. *What moral principles are involved?* In this case the dominant principle was beneficence—doing good for others. But also, the leader must ask herself if there are any morally debatable aspects to the choice she makes. The ethical question I asked myself that day was: To what degree is it feasible to risk a human life to do good for others? I decided to ask Presley to make a risky exercise in courage because of the potential benefits for many people.

5. *How would these principles be advanced or violated by each alternative action?* A leader thinks through each choice and its potential results. If we had not advanced to the bridge, we would not have been doing our jobs. We would not have been helping the greatest number. I knew from the beginning that

my commitment to morality would entail costs at times. Because I had earlier in life convinced myself of the greater good of a moral life—largely due to my training at West Point—I chose the moral course and mustered the personal courage to take responsibility for the actions I chose.

I don't know how Presley arrived at *his* decision. In all frankness, this driver-mechanic had previously distinguished himself to his supervisors primarily for his individual unkemptness. But in my eyes his decision turned him into a hero. In a single courageous act, he fulfilled his highest function as a human being by helping thousands of people.

CHARACTER IS A PREREQUISITE FOR GREATNESS

West Point teaches the lessons of character over and over again, in ways both bold and subtle. One story the cadets are told has deep roots in the history of our nation and of the Academy. It is really two entwined stories of men who, during the American Revolutionary War, distinguished themselves by their brilliant leadership of soldiers—generals George Washington and Benedict Arnold—men whose stories make plain the virtue of choosing the harder right.

In the early days of the war, both men showed extraordinary skill, courage, and heroism. Of Arnold's victory at Bemis Heights, leading to the British surrender at Saratoga, the historian Herman Beukema reluctantly acknowledged, "The laurels for one of the decisive victories of all history rest on Arnold's brow."

But only one of the two men stayed the course through the dark, discouraging days of the war, having the personal character to persevere in the face of overwhelming difficulty. The other man collapsed under pressure and sought to sell the British the plans for the strategically key fortresses he commanded at West Point—which had been built and supplied to maintain control of the Hudson River, vital to the security of New York. Fortunately, Washington discovered Arnold's treacherous plot before the damage was done (although Arnold himself escaped).

Of the two men, one is revered as the father of his country; the other is a man without a country, his name remembered only as a synonym for treason.

At West Point, Washington is honored in numerous ways. The most prominent memorial is seen by cadets three times daily. In front of the Cadet Dining Hall, in the center of the Plain, stands a larger-than-life statue of the general on horseback, elevated by a ten-foot-high pedestal. It is quite intentional that he is featured at the very center of the grand stage formed by the campus buildings and the surrounding mountains.

Arnold is remembered, too—in stark terms that remind us all how much rests on a leader's character. On the east wall of the old cadet chapel, located in the West Point cemetery, hangs a collection of plaques naming the senior officers of the Revolutionary War. At the front in the most prominent position, as one would expect, is Washington's plaque. Concluding the collection, in an inconspicuous position at the rear of the building, hangs a mysterious plaque bearing only the words "Major General," followed by a chiseled blank space where a name would have been carved, then a date of birth,

"1741," and another chiseled blank space where the date of death would have been carved. Arnold's plaque represents the symbolic obliteration of his name from the honor rolls of American history.

LEADERS OF CHARACTER CREATE ORGANIZATIONS OF CHARACTER

Just as individual leaders manifest depth of character, so also do organizations. I can illustrate what I mean by "organizations of character" by parallel examples found in the recent history of American business.

Not long ago, Johnson & Johnson's organizational character was tested in an extreme manner when one of its most popular products, Tylenol, was found to have been tainted by tampering. Like some other successful companies, Johnson & Johnson has a credo that defines its essential values. Simple statements specify its responsibilities to customers, communities, employees, and stockholders—in that order.

Adherence to its credo—first priority to the safety and health of its customers—enabled the company to react decisively to the crisis without hesitation, by immediately recalling the entire nationwide inventory of the product. This was carried out despite the loss of $240 million, i.e., at the risk of corporate survival.

Johnson & Johnson was an example of an organization of character—living by its espoused values, even at times when it was not only difficult, but potentially disastrous.

Not long after the Johnson & Johnson incident, nearly

one hundred thousand pounds of deadly methyl isocyanate gas leaked from a Union Carbide plant in Bhopal, India, killing over three thousand people. Eventually, tens of thousands suffered permanent damage from the leak, and hundreds of thousands temporary damage.

Immediately following the misfortune, Warren Anderson, Union Carbide's chairman at the time, flew to Bhopal and said he would devote the rest of his career to resolving the problems caused by the accident. The company sent $1 million in emergency relief, and its U.S. employees collected and sent another $150,000.

However, the company soon backpedaled. A year later, Anderson told *Business Week*, "I overreacted." He explained that the litigation against Union Carbide initiated in India "could drag on for five or more years. That's our way of life in America. I'm not going to play dead." Indeed, the legal proceedings lasted nearly five years, until 1989, when it was decided that Union Carbide would have to pay $470 million in damages. (Due to other legal problems, distribution of the money did not begin until late 1992.)

I am not aware whether Union Carbide has a clear statement of values, as Johnson & Johnson does. But the company's first action—its chairman flying to Bhopal and vowing to devote his career to resolving the problems of the accident —is some indication of what it perceived as appropriate company values. However, when the cost became too high, Union Carbide failed to follow through on those values. My point is that an organization should be clear about what its values are, and be willing to live up to them—even when it is very costly.

To have taken responsibility for all the damage of this

tremendous disaster might have been financially catastrophic for Union Carbide. Yet that is precisely what Johnson & Johnson did in its time of trouble. In the end, it turned out well for the latter company, because the stand it took built consumer confidence in its products. But even if it had not turned out well, the company's action was still the choice that an organization of character should have made—the harder right.

In the Union Carbide case, we cannot predict whether paying all the damages promptly would have had equally positive results. What we can say, however, is that the company's hesitation to make reparations marked the beginning of a long period of struggle for the organization—including a serious takeover bid, sales of assets, and mass reorganization—from which Union Carbide has yet to emerge.

Between Union Carbide and Johnson & Johnson, one showed superior organizational character.

Because a young soldier named Presley chose the harder right, my engineering company repaired a damaged bridge and restored many lives to normalcy in a provincial region of Vietnam. In a small way, I had an opportunity to reward Presley's demonstration of character.

Before he returned to the States at the end of his tour, he came to me and said, "Sir, in a little while I'll be leaving the Army and going home. But I sure would be proud to go home as a Specialist 5 instead of a Specialist 4."

He was asking me for a promotion, which had been previously denied to him by his sergeants because he was not as clean, well groomed, or knowledgeable as other soldiers in my company. Remembering what he and I had been through, I dismissed him and called in my first sergeant. "Top," I said, "I want to promote Presley." I listened briefly to the first sergeant's protests. Then I said quietly, "Top, promote Presley."

He went home a Specialist 5. I have never seen or heard from him again, but I will always remember him fondly as a soldier of character.

If a nation is to be a nation of character, it must have many organizations of character. Such organizations are almost always headed by leaders of character. This is the reason that it is not merely leaders that West Point seeks to develop, but leaders of character.

6

Learning to Be a Team Member

During their first daunting year at West Point, plebes pursue one and the same goal: to be such exemplary followers that they can avoid the unwanted attention of the upperclass cadets whose incessant corrections and memorization assignments make plebes' lives difficult. Plebes work together with strength and determination to defeat this common "enemy." The key to survival is, as plebes say, to "cooperate and graduate" which translates into a respect for communal information. The plebes will, for example, team up against the upperclass cadets in the distribution of the daily "poop"—the information they must recite on command, which changes every day (the current movie playing, the menu in the dining hall, the number of days until upcoming events). Plebes learn that they can share information on the Academy-wide computer network to save themselves time and energy. One cadet can copy the week's menu from the dining hall and upload it from his computer, saving one thousand other plebes the effort of going to the dining hall to copy the menu. This is "cooperate and graduate" in action.

Shared values and shared goals, particularly the honor code, form the foundation for successful teamwork. The importance of sharing is reinforced as often as possible. For cadets, there are no individual incentives, only team incentives. If a team member shows up on time for inspection with his belt buckle polished, his shoes shined, and his plebe knowledge perfectly memorized—but other members of his team show up late—not only is he not rewarded for his individual achievement, he is berated, even punished, for abandoning his team when they needed his help.

After a number of experiences like this, working for the good of one's peers becomes a way of life. In learning to be a member of a team, cadets experience the positive side of team membership. They see that belonging to a group makes each individual more powerful, not smaller or anonymous or dependent. Dependency in West Point terms is a good thing—as long as you and others mutually depend upon one another to multiply your collective strength. This approach is in contrast to some leadership programs which decry submission to team goals as limiting and promote the skills of acting alone.

The Academy tries to create team situations in real work environments similar to those cadets will experience during their careers as soldiers. At Camp Buckner, a sparsely furnished, permanent camp facility on the shores of Lake Popolopen, twelve miles from the Academy's main grounds, cadets spend six weeks of intensive field exercises designed to convey—as dramatically as possible—the requirements teamwork.

Cadets who come to Buckner have spent the past year learning from ground zero who they are. Some emerge from this intense experience feeling invincible—for having been mentally and physically rugged enough to have stayed the ego-pounding course. During their summer vacations, however, they come to discover that few outsiders—neither friends nor folks back home—understand what plebe year was like. No one, in fact, quite understands, except for their fellow West Pointers. Nothing stimulates teamwork as much as shared, intensely personal, group experiences. This is the basis of a powerful group identity that stays with Academy graduates all their lives.

There is a lot more to teamwork than the fact that "many hands make light work." Teams can do things that individuals could never accomplish. The cadet's experience at Buckner is carefully contrived to give each cadet the opportunity to feel the enormous power of teamwork. We can talk endlessly about the way teamwork multiplies the power of individuals, but there is nothing quite like experiencing this astonishing synergy in action.

OBSTACLES TO TEAMWORK

Trust is the glue that holds a team together. A leader forgets this at his own peril. If we can make it perfectly clear to leaders-in-training that there are many instances in life where you must entrust your destiny to someone else, we've

...ore about teamwork than any assignment or ...ill ever teach them.

...situation: Early in their stay at Buckner, the ...t out in teams of six on the leadership obstacle course. This exercise is designed to raise in the cadets' minds the fundamental obstacles to teamwork and to give them some practice at group problem solving. The first obstacle is a four-level platform with nine feet between each rung. Each cadet must climb to the top and back down again. No guidelines whatsoever are offered on how to accomplish this task, but it is very obvious to the cadets as they stand and gaze up at the platform that whatever they have to do, they have to do it together.

In this context, two roadblocks to successful teamwork recur again and again: 1) *technical problems*—in the case of our first team crisis, how to get from the ground to the top of the platform (the team boosts up the tallest member who then reaches down and helps everyone else climb up), and (2) *human dynamics problems*—in this case how to compensate for individual weaknesses, say a shorter or heavier cadet, how to make sure that everyone's ideas for solving the problem are heard, and how to choose the best solution, all the while retaining enthusiasm for the task at hand and good group spirit.

LEADERS' RESPONSIBILITY AND CLASSIC PITFALLS

It is surprising how many leaders forget that the high performance of their team is their own responsibility. Instead, they blindly expect the concatenation of the team's members to naturally produce results. While nearly all managers either pay lip service to teamwork, or honestly believe that they head teams which function strongly, in fact few achieve genuinely high performance. In their book *Spectacular Teamwork*, authors Robert Blake, Jane Mouton, and Robert Allen found that two out of three managers initially rated themselves highly when asked if their teams performed strongly. However, after feedback from their team members, only one in eight maintained the previous optimistic estimation.

The greatest obstacles to truly high-performing teamwork usually are in the minds of the leaders themselves, whose misconceptions can lead to techniques that impede rather than encourage teamwork. There are four classic pitfalls that many leaders are unfortunately prone to:

✳ *The autonomy syndrome.* Many leaders believe that they alone must have the solution to every problem, the answer to every question. Not only do they thus create impossible pressure on themselves, they cheat themselves out of the valuable input of their subordinates. Simply by definition, the autonomous manager clearly discourages teamwork.

✳ *The paranoia syndrome.* Many leaders jealously guard management data as if they were TOP SECRET Pentagon documents, for fear that someone will exploit the information against them. For managers to be able to elicit from their subordinates the knowledgeable and complete input that will make them high-performance team members, a clear flow of information is necessary.

✳ *The bully syndrome.* Some managers believe they have to "rough people up" verbally or emotionally to get them to perform. While this may work on a few employees, many more will become overly stressed or panicked, and ultimately alienated. If these problems are prevalent among a team's members, the progress of the entire team will be impeded and discouraged.

❋ *The "every man for himself" syndrome.* A manager may naively believe that if every employee simply does his job, everything will work out fine—no matter how his work affects the big picture, or his colleagues. This approach can never achieve synergy. Only when each individual feels a part of a distinct, more meaningful goal can high performance be achieved.

EMPOWERING THE TEAM

The most effective leaders understand the power of a highly productive team working with them. Weak leaders think of their team members as merely extensions of their own hands and feet.

I once worked with a general who was willing to trust people to do their jobs just from general guidance through occasional staff meetings. He gave subordinates complete areas of responsibility as subdivisions of his own, and gave them the freedom to execute their responsibilities with considerable autonomy.

A few years later, he was succeeded by a bright leader who was a workaholic—brilliant, aggressive, and ambitious, but without appreciation for his subordinates. The people who worked for him were primarily treated as "gofers"—"go fer this," "go fer that." Rather than giving them missions to accomplish and the freedom to decide how to do them, he simply prescribed one task after another. His subordinates were merely added sets of hands and feet for him to do his bidding. His best subordinates were so miserable that he drove them away, and he had to replace them with lesser people who were willing to be mere gofers.

How does a leader empower the members of the team to perform at their best? Here are a few guidelines (some suggested by Blake, Mouton, and Allen):

＊ The leader of a high-performance team begins with the basis of a high regard for the team members. This includes an open mind and true two-way communication, including the patience to listen to even their wildest ideas about how to achieve company goals.

＊ The leader of a high-performance team elicits the team members' commitment by enabling them to share in the organization's success. While the most obvious way to share in success is financial, the team's success can also be measured morally or practically—say, the success of efficiently and inexpensively making a good product that is beneficial to the community. Team member satisfaction arises from contributing to that success.

＊ A leader can set (or, even better, lead his team to set) collective goals for the team. Stressing that their individual evaluations will be interpreted through the success of the achievement of collective goals, members of the team will have to work together to achieve those goals.

＊ The leader of a high-performance team encourages members to participate jointly in analyzing problems and offering solutions. He fosters open communication so differences among members can be worked through to improve shared understanding.

✳ When the leader of a high-performance team gives directions, he also provides opportunities to clarify matters in case they are not understood. As a result, everyone is sure of what is to be done and why.

✳ Through establishing open communication, a leader creates an environment in which team members are willing to mutually assist one another, reflecting the team's cohesion and loyalty. Similarly, through open communication, a leader will enable team members to address internal conflicts explicitly, and openly attempt to locate the underlying cause.

✳ Team member performance evaluations use criteria that have already been agreed upon jointly by leaders and team members. During the evaluation process, communication is two-way.

COLLECTIVE GOALS THAT BUILD GREAT TEAMS

Just as the plebe cadets build their team to deal with the common enemy of the upperclass cadets, one of the Academy's strategies is to invent a common enemy for teams to battle. This reinforces group cohesion.

Collective goals are not necessarily inspiring to every member of a team at any given moment. The challenge for a leader is to find a way to convince all team members to work together—to inspire her team. A leader can motivate the team through an *artificial* goal when the members are not particularly moved by the most obvious goal. This requires inventing—or redefining—the enemy. Let me explain.

For one exercise at Buckner, cadets combine into platoon-sized teams of about thirty-five people to rapidly assemble portable bridges (like the one Presley and I built in Vietnam), which are built in the span of a few hours—an impossible task without teamwork. The panels and girders which are the basic building blocks of the modular-designed portable bridges each weigh several hundred pounds; simply to lift one requires a team.

In wartime, such bridges are usually assembled with a specific and immediate goal—to restore vital commerce, to get away from the enemy, or to get closer to attack him. These life-or-death situations organically create urgency. However, with no such goal in mind, it can be difficult to inspire cadets to the appropriate spirit for moving about eight-hundred-pound girders.

Therefore, an artificial goal is established. The "enemy" is redefined. The platoons compete to see who can complete the bridge in the shortest time. This motivation is not dissimilar from the corporate world, where the employees at Reebok are told that beating Nike is their goal, or Avis's long-standing battle to try to capture Hertz's position as "number one."

This is *functional* competition. It works because its end is a goal whose achievement is important not just to each individual in the group, but to the group collectively. However, leaders sometimes set up situations of *dysfunctional* competition by creating goals in which members of the team are forced to compete against each other for bonuses or promotion. Not only does this kind of competition present many team members with conflicts of loyalty, it rewards them for individual excellence, and not team excellence.

GAINING CONFIDENCE IN THE GROUP, NOT JUST IN ONESELF

By the time Camp Buckner comes to a close, not only have the cadets achieved various group goals, they have also learned to appreciate the power of teamwork. Perhaps most importantly, they have forged a group identity. This identity is bolstered by a West Point ritual. Before the end of their stay at Buckner, the cadets road-march under full packs to Lake Popolopen, where they negotiate one more confidence course, which includes the notorious "slide for life." This, the most famous thrill ride at West Point, requires the cadets to climb an eighty-foot ladder to the top of a tower, and then descend by gripping a hand-trolley attached to a steel cable, which extends downward from the tower across the lake. Supporting their entire weight with their arms, the cadets ride the trolley, and then drop into the water just before reaching the far shore. Clambering out of the water, they climb a pole and walk across a log suspended twenty-five feet in the air, then crawl out on a rope stretched above the water and, on command, let go of the rope, plunging into the lake below. When they drag their bodies out of the water, the cadets' most severe test of self-confidence is over.

Similar to the effect of Beast Barracks, Camp Buckner enables cadets to experience an exponential increase in self-confidence as the harsh demands of the summer are met. This increase is then reinforced symbolically by West Point. The summer closes with a twelve-mile road march back to the main cadet area, where the yearlings are greeted on the Plain by the Superintendent and other well-wishers, who congratulate them on a job well done.

There is also tangible reinforcement. At the end of this ceremony, the Superintendent promotes each to the rank of cadet corporal. In the Army, the rank of corporal is the lowest enlisted rank in which one exercises leadership of other soldiers. For the cadet the promotion is meaningful. As the saying goes, that which is hardest earned is most appreciated; this first promotion represents more than a year of hard work to each cadet. By the promotion, the institution publicly marks its trust in the cadets' ability to assume roles of leadership over the cadets junior to them in rank. During the coming year they will be given the job of team leader within their squad, which assigns them responsibility for leading one or two plebes.

SECOND PASS:

Positioning the Individual

Inside the Group

7

Just and Unjust Leadership

The first major lesson leaders must learn is to follow. The next is to trust and be trustworthy. Contradictory as it might seem, the third lesson is independence of mind.

There are times when leaders need to be able to stand tall before their peers, their subordinates, and their own leaders—times when they need to stand up to authority, to say "No" or "I disagree" or "I think your proposal spells disaster."

The Academy does not seek to build egoism in leaders. It doesn't want arrogant leaders who insist they're right at any cost, but rather leaders who have a sense of judgment of when to follow and when to question. This is why the Academy teaches self-command and teamwork, which create powerful bonds between the individual and the organization, before it teaches independence.

Independence of mind is taught at West Point in several

venues, including a particularly challenging course in moral philosophy. One of the texts used for this course is *Just and Unjust Wars* by Michael Walzer. In addition to his academic and authorial credentials, Walzer was a Vietnam-era peace activist. The book grew out of his desire to resolve the troubling issues of that war which affected him and many others of his generation—including West Pointers. This book is a groundbreaker in the study of war; no modern moral theorist has so cogently articulated just-war theory with specific historical lessons for those who may make war in the future. Year by year, West Point is probably the most substantial buyer of Walzer's book.

In the study of this book, the Academy draws the cadets into critically examining the moral issues raised by U.S. military history and policy. This kind of scrutiny forces cadets at times to call into question the mission, and even the sense of themselves, that brought them to the Academy in the first place. The equivalent would be business schools offering courses to question the value of capitalism, or to debate whether routine business practices can be justified.

Why does the Academy think it a good idea to elevate the cadets' sensitivity to moral issues of going to war and fighting wars? Why should leaders think about the basic morality of their situations? It's crucial because leadership entails having a mind broad enough to sense when the organization is wrong and a heart courageous enough to do something to fix it.

TO TEACH INDEPENDENCE OF MIND, WE STUDY FAILURE

When MBA candidates study business failures to better understand leadership, it is usually in practical terms, not ethical ones. I think the moral examination of one's business— war, in cadets' case—receives an unusual degree of emphasis at West Point. I can't help wonder if, say, financial institutions whose managers were indicted for insider trading wouldn't have benefited from a more self-critical education.

If I were to apply the West Point method to teaching ethics to business students, I would begin by teaching an introduction to both logic and the primary themes in moral philosophy to equip the students better for engaging in moral reasoning. Then I would look for historical case studies of actual situations in business which illustrate the spectrum of moral challenges and lapses that can occur. If I were dealing with students who were all from one industry or business firm I would look for those case study situations which arise for employees within that industry. In fact, employees within the industry may be the best source for discovering what those morally troublesome situations are. The more closely we can make the hypothetical situations resemble actual situations with which the students have dealt or will deal, the more fruitful will be the discussion and the more powerful will be their engagement with the moral dilemmas and their ability to make relevant connections to their own work. Following is an example used with cadets. It is a situation taken from the past but one in which any young, future second lieutenant fresh out of West Point could conceivably find himself.

The situation is presented in *Just and Unjust Wars* and is used to provoke the cadets to think critically in moral terms about a particularly difficult chapter in the Army's history: the war in Vietnam.

In one chapter Walzer describes the official practice of American units in "free fire zones" answering small-arms fire from Vietnamese villages with artillery and air strikes on the villages themselves—which caused heavy civilian casualties and extensive destruction. Walzer argues that American leaders had a moral obligation to accept greater risks to soldiers, in order to impose fewer risks upon noncombatant Vietnamese civilians.

This notion usually provokes an outcry from cadets in the class discussion. While only one may verbalize this reaction, many others will agree with him. "Come on, sir, don't you think that Walzer sounds like a pinko liberal worrying about the villagers? War's hell and if they shoot at me, I'm gonna unload on them with all I've got! Nuke 'em till they glow!"

Through my questions I try to elicit the other side: that while the soldier's job is to take risks, the noncombatant has a right to a reasonable degree of protection. Aren't there alternative methods for stopping the sniper than strafing the entire village? A door-to-door search is suggested by one cadet —but then rejected out-of-hand by another.

"Why should I risk the lives of my soldiers that way, sir? They could get shot by the sniper the minute they walk through the door! Aren't my men's lives my primary responsibility?"

"Sure," I reply, but then I ask if also there are any *other* people in this scenario to whom he has a responsibility. Grudgingly, he admits that he has a duty to the noncombatant villagers under the Geneva and Hague conventions (and as fellow human beings).

The complications of the Vietnam war then emerge: that in many places and times it was a guerrilla war; that the enemy often wore no uniform; that many noncombatants sympathized with the Vietcong. These spur other cadets to argue against the villagers' protection. "Sir, if they weren't sympathizers with the VC, then why weren't they in the pacification camps?"

Through discussion they realize it's not that simple. There weren't nearly enough pacification camps for the non-sympathizers. Other noncombatants were *forced* to harbor VC. I also raise another issue that further confuses the already conflicted cadets: "Let's say you're a villager forced against your will to protect a sniper, who one day fires a couple of rounds out of the window of your hootch at some U.S. soldiers in the distance. The next thing you know your entire village is leveled by artillery, and your wife and children are killed along with two dozen other villagers. The VC survives and says, 'See how much the Americans care about you? Join up with me and help drive them out of our country!' Aren't you more likely to cooperate voluntarily with the VC after that?"

"I guess so, sir."

"So is it possible that *your* tactics, while in the narrowest sense protecting your soldiers, are actually making the war more dangerous for them by angering the local population and turning them against you?"

"Yes, sir . . . I guess so."

Many of them come to appreciate the wisdom of Walzer's argument. Others don't. Some steadfastly maintain that as military officers they wouldn't be responsible for strategy adopted in Washington—only to keep their soldiers alive. But they all have been morally and intellectually challenged by the discussion. They have learned what some of the important considerations will be should they be faced with similar dilemmas in the future.

I found myself in a position similar to the cadets' when, several years after the Vietnam war ended, I attended the Army's Command and General Staff College. Among the required reading was Jeffrey Race's book *War Comes to Long An* —which inspired the chapter in Walzer's book I just described. This forced me to begin to think more critically about the U.S.'s role—as well as my own—in Vietnam.

For the first time, I began to doubt that the U.S.'s espoused strategy—pacification and winning "the hearts and minds" of the local people—was ever taken seriously or implemented in any way that had a chance of succeeding. Instead, as I hope my class illustrates to the cadets, U.S. tactics in Vietnam may have worked contrary to the stated strategy and appears to have doomed the U.S. effort to failure. Such a possibility—valid or not—is a staggering prospect for anyone who risked his life and lost numerous close buddies in Vietnam.

But, at least, it is to the Army's credit that the institution itself began a process of self-correction that touched me at Command and General Staff College, and continues to touch the cadets every year. The fruit of this self-critical process was visible in the conduct of the U.S. leaders and soldiers during the 1991 war in the Gulf to restore Kuwaiti sovereignty.

Another class deals with Walzer's conclusion that the U.S. Army has its strongest moral grounds for war when it fights to right wrongs that are committed against those who cannot defend themselves against those wrongs. Or, in other words, we are at our best when using military force only to defeat aggression.

The cadets felt the strength of this idea when they listened to Elie Wiesel lecture. Soon after the Nobel Prize-winning author began to speak, he peered into the audience, and on examining the sea of uniformed youths, decided to veer from his prepared notes.

Looking upon his assembly, he said he couldn't help but be reminded of the first time he had ever seen a U.S. soldier. By the time American troops arrived to liberate Auschwitz, the young Wiesel had turned into a mere shell of a human being, barely able to raise himself up on his elbows. The first soldier to enter the cell block where he had been detained, recounted Wiesel, was an enormous black man in a green uniform, who was followed by several of his colleagues.

Wiesel said he remembered looking at the black man's face and how his eyes peered around the cell with a look of disgust. He was so revulsed by what he saw—by the evidence of the cruelty that had been imposed upon his fellow human beings—that he began cursing. That cursing, said Wiesel, "was the sweetest sound I ever heard."

DOERS WHO THINK

Through classroom instruction and lectures as described above the Academy broadens the cadets' moral reach, giving them the intellectual training to distinguish right from wrong in complex situations. But the process doesn't stop with intellectual accomplishment. West Point's mission is to train "doers who think." Leaders have not succeeded if they only perceive injustice. They must act to correct it. In the Third Pass, we show the cadets how to stand up in the face of injustice. The faculty plays a key role in this process.

In each case, instructors have some experience performing their discipline. Teachers of military history have helped to make history in the latest U.S. engagements. Teachers of international relations have worked on the formulation of U.S. foreign policy. English composition teachers have been engaged around the world as public affairs staff officers. The faculty brings a rich lode of practical experience to the classroom.

There are other advantages as well. While the majority of the instructors do not bring long years of faculty experience to their teaching, neither are they stale, tired, bored, or cynical, as are some of their counterparts in civilian universities. Their opportunity to concentrate on teaching, unencumbered by the normal academic pressures of research and publishing, tends to energize and invigorate their classes, as well as free them to be accessible to cadets for extra work on scholastic matters. (Indeed, cadets theoretically have twenty-four-hour access to their teachers, who usually provide their classes with their home telephone numbers.) They also provide a great deal of volunteer labor to support extracurricular activities.

The Academy faculty also serves to broaden the cadets whose narrow conception of a commanding military officer may be too visceral to include being an intellectual. Making the opposite point, a favorite story among West Point instructors is that when the macho West Pointer George Patton first saw Rommel approaching his forces across the desert, he did *not* say, "Rommel, I'm going to whip you!" Rather, he yelled exultantly, "Rommel, you ☆!?*&! *I read your book!*"

In the classroom, the cadets come to see the world beyond West Point as infinitely more complex than they had previously imagined. Until this point, their challenge as emerging leaders has been to make themselves into competent and reliable members of a group. Now they realize that more is required. Good leaders, the kind of leaders they want to become, must be outstanding individuals as well, having the wisdom and the courage to stand alone when necessary. The next phase of leadership training, direct leadership, requires the cadets to stand alone in a somewhat different context—as team leaders. The plebes in their charge rely on them for everything from professional instruction to personal advice and, as a consequence, the cadet team leaders' daily lives at West Point become vastly more complex as well.

8

Face-to-Face Leadership

There is a wide gulf between setting a goal for a group of people and getting it done. This gulf is precisely what a direct, or face-to-face, leader must cross—because in direct leadership the central task is the effective influence of other people, face-to-face, to get a job done.

Second-year cadets find themselves in this position as team leaders. A West Point team leader is given direct responsibility for the progress of one to three plebes. In time, he learns that the challenge of direct leadership is to care both for accomplishing the goal *and* for the people who accomplish it.

For almost all cadets, being a team leader is their first experience in having such an enormous amount of immediate influence over someone else. A former cadet I know carries in his wallet a prayer that is a brief ethic for direct leaders:

Care more than others think is wise
Risk more than others think is safe
Dream more than others think is practical
Expect more than others think is possible.

CARE MORE THAN OTHERS
THINK IS WISE

There are many, varied styles that leaders use to influence their followers. Some are soft-spoken while others shout; some are dramatic, or understated, or dour, or funny. But with any of these styles of interaction it is still possible for leaders to show that they care—or that they don't. The greatest challenge leaders face is to show that they care deeply about both accomplishing the mission *and* the people who accomplish it.

The leader's true effectiveness arises largely from a sincere regard for each member of the team. General Omar Bradley wrote, "A leader should possess human understanding and consideration for others. People are not robots and should not be treated as such. I do not by any means suggest coddling. But people are intelligent, complicated beings who will respond favorably to human understanding and consideration. By these means their leader will get maximum effort from each of them. He will also get loyalty."

In their first experiences of direct leadership, cadet team leaders encounter what they perceive as a dilemma: wanting to maintain a positive relationship with their subordinates, but at the same time wanting to demand high standards of performance. Some mistakenly presume that the quest of caring for their subordinates means they must slacken performance standards to keep the relationship positive. Not understanding how to do both, some become soft and try too hard to please; while others feel they must adopt a cold, remote approach to lead effectively.

The tension between mission accomplishment and the needs of subordinates is ever-present for leaders. Most good ones find a way to tend to both. Among cadets, these leaders are the ones who genuinely believe, and are able to convey to their subordinates, that the high standards they demand are a reflection of their genuine interest in the subordinates' success as cadets. For them, attaining the mission and meeting subordinates' needs are melded into one.

During my plebe year, I was particularly aware of the constant corrections of my appearance and behavior by a yearling named Mark Sheridan. At first, I perceived his attention as sheer harassment arising from some inexplicable malice on his part. One day, however, he stopped to talk with me about my dietary habits and made several suggestions for my well-being. From then on, I began to change my opinion about Cadet Sheridan, believing that he hadn't been harassing me at all. Rather, he was doggedly working to make me a good cadet. That was also what I wanted. When I finally realized that his high standards would help me to succeed, I was inspired to try my best to fulfill his expectations.

Another example—provided by a great wartime leader—is that of William Tecumseh Sherman, West Point class of 1841. Called "the first modern general" by his biographer, Sir Basil Liddell Hart, Sherman was clearly considerate of his men. He marched them at night to spare them the burning sun, and he rode in the fields beside the columns of troops to avoid forcing soldiers off the road.

Even more important, Sherman's men learned quickly that the extremes he demanded of them actually saved them many casualties. According to Liddell Hart, Sherman was able to demand so much from his men—they would march for him at a moment's notice and subsist on the scantiest of rations—because he took care of them on the battlefield. His men had a supreme faith in his ability to keep them alive, and so when he called on them to fight they did so with great confidence. In short, Sherman's consideration of his men made them all the more successful in achieving their mission.

On a much smaller scale, I was less successful in resolving this same dilemma in Vietnam. In order to finish the urgent construction of an airfield, I was working my soldiers for ten- and twelve-hour days, six and a half days a week. I was quickly wearing them down to such a state of exhaustion that they were becoming less productive (and more miserable) than they would have been had I eased up a bit. I see now that I could ask that kind of sacrifice from them only for a high cause and for a relatively brief time.

On the other hand, I still recall vividly how much I cared for those soldiers like Presley. Another was the young lieutenant, Layne Maney, who was badly wounded by the first mortar round when my company was attacked. It took me ninety minutes to get a chopper to take him to a hospital, and even with first aid, he nearly died en route to Cam Ranh Bay. When I looked him up years later, he told me he had experienced two more close brushes with death. But he survived, and after eighteen months of operations, his body had been pieced back together and he continued with his Army career. I still have a feeling of sharing, vicariously, in his victory over death that day.

Leaders soon discover that subordinates come in all shapes, sizes, colors, temperaments, and levels of skill. General Creighton Abrams advised, "Build on what a man is, don't tear him down."

"Building on what a man is" implies on the part of leaders their undertaking to become thoroughly acquainted with their subordinates, to figure out what strengths they each possess. Roughly, subordinates can be divided into three groups, each of which requires a different approach from their leader.

✳ *Knows her job well and is motivated to do it well.* By the end of plebe year, most plebes—like many employees—have become very good at managing their tasks with minimal supervision and they need little management, frequently, nothing more than a bit of guidance and occasional praise. These are the employees who make an organization hum.

✳ *Motivated to succeed but job skills are below par.* Although this kind of subordinate, often a new employee, requires additional time and attention, his eagerness to do well is more important than his lack of skill. While he needs patient and detailed training, and his work will have to be checked frequently—at least in the beginning—there is good reason to believe that, shown a little patience, he will develop into a high performer.

✳ *Job knowledge and skills are clearly acceptable, but lacks motivation to succeed at job.* It has been said that leaders spend 90 percent of their time attending to the problems of 10 percent of the work force. Subordinates with motivational problems are the most difficult for a leader to work with.

Empathetic listening to such subordinates by leaders is the surest way to uncover the missing source of motivation. It is usually an unfulfilled need in the person's life, which, according to research psychologist Clayton Alderfer, usually falls into one of three categories:

1. *Basic existence needs*. If a subordinate is having trouble providing the basic necessities for himself and his family, for example due to low pay or poor financial mismanagement, the leader may need to arrange for the employee to receive counseling—in this case, on setting up and living within a budget.

2. *Relationship needs*. If the subordinate has human relationship problems inside or outside the workplace, they can detract from his job performance, and again the leader might try to seek counseling for him.

3. *Personal growth needs*. If he feels his job is unfulfilling or unsatisfying, there are various ways to attempt to enrich it for him—increasing his level of responsibility; combining tasks; forming natural work units; removing some of his supervision (while retaining accountability) if he needs more independence.

As we mentioned in an earlier chapter, it is the responsibility of the leader to set both the moral tone and the standards of performance for the team. The leader clarifies the criteria for what is acceptable and what is unacceptable, and provides an open atmosphere that encourages hard work and creative problem solving among the group.

Essential to stimulating the group toward high performance and high morale is open communication. As we learned earlier, one of the basic skills of followership is listening to orders and then carrying them out. However, a leader has the obligation to initiate and to foster two-way communication, because this is his best method of becoming acquainted with his subordinates, their strengths and weaknesses, and the unique contributions they can offer his team.

Effective listening to others is a skill that must be acquired by thoughtful practice. A few fundamental techniques can make a big difference: Ask subordinates open-ended questions in which a yes or a no won't do for an answer, in the hopes of drawing them out. Let them complete their thoughts. Maintain eye contact. Repeat or rephrase what they've said and carry it to the next question, especially reflecting your understanding of the emotion that they are feeling as they talk. For example, "You mean you're feeling frustrated by this situation?"

RISK MORE THAN OTHERS THINK IS SAFE

Leaders accept honest mistakes by subordinates. We all learn from our mistakes—unless leaders create an atmosphere in which mistakes cannot be survived.

A story about Thomas Watson, Jr., dramatizes this point. IBM lost $10 million due to the mistake of a subordinate, who immediately handed in his resignation in shame. Watson rejected it categorically. "Not on your life!" he said. "You think I'll let you go now after spending $10 million on your education?"

That is a healthy attitude for leaders. So long as subordinates learn from their mistakes so the mistakes are not repeated, leaders gain by tolerating honest errors.

For a short time the Army had a program called "Zero Defects," in which redoubled attention to detail was supposed to ensure that no mistakes would ever be made. Of course, it was not successful. Worst of all, Zero Defects completely oppressed the freedom of soldiers to be adventurous, to be creative, to take risks. The program was eventually dropped.

MANAGING SUBORDINATES' STRESS

Direct leaders need to understand and manage the stress which they impose on subordinates. Stress develops in an individual any time a gap appears between what is demanded of her and what she perceives she is capable of doing. If a plebe is asked to render a hand salute and she has never done one before, she will probably feel stress, but if she has been in the Army before and knows how to salute, she will not.

A little bit of stress can actually enhance a subordinate's performance by arousing all his senses to peak performance. But excessive stress can be counterproductive. Asking clearly more than a person is capable of, or adding artificial urgency, such as yelling at plebes, can make them less able to perform well. Years ago, on R-Day, plebes were greeted with much more of this artificial pressure. Today they are not, and the

Academy has found that they learn to perform their tasks (saluting, marching, wearing their uniforms properly) much more quickly.

To properly manage stress, leaders usually break down complex tasks into small, manageable increments which permit the subordinate small successes. Such increments impose productive levels of stress and accelerate the learning process.

The experience of the plebe year enables plebes to subsequently handle stress in many similar situations. For example, some West Point graduates go on to Airborne school, where, like all the recruits, they are objects of hectoring by the sergeants. The former cadets are not fazed by it—it rolls off their backs, which only makes the sergeants feel frustrated. The cadets' experience in plebe year teaches them that they are fully capable of handling this kind of treatment, so they do not feel stress.

PUNISH WHEN NECESSARY

"Once you try everything you know and it doesn't work, then what do you do?" asked a team leader who was stymied when one of his plebes behaved as if he were exempt from the many rules at West Point. He thought he could get away with breaking the regulations, and break them he did. After morning inspection, he went back to bed. He refused to do his share of room chores. He kept contraband—in this case a Walkman—in his room.

The team leader at first tried to get the other two members of the offending cadet's team to settle the problem among themselves. This strategy bore no fruit. Indeed, the plebe told his roommates that there was nothing that the upperclass cadets could do to get him to follow the rules.

At this point, the team leader knew that the time for positive encouragement was over, and the time for punishment had begun. He began to scrutinize the plebe at a microscopic level. Corrections, for instance, were made repeatedly in the way he made his bed, resulting in its being torn apart each morning so he would have to do it over. He was a frequent target for the recitation of plebe knowledge, and extra attention was paid to inspect whether his shoes were shined, his belt buckle polished, his gig line straight.

He was given the position of room orderly so that he alone became responsible for each infraction in the room—whether he or one of his roommates actually made it.

As the cadet reacted to such pressures, his plebe peers kept haranguing him. Interestingly, I think the pressure that they exerted on him had even more effect than the treatment he received from the upperclass cadets. In the end, he became conscientious enough to deflect the attentions of both his peers and his direct leaders.

MAKING PUNISHMENT EFFECTIVE

For face-to-face leaders, punishment should be the last resort, only because it's the least effective means of altering a subordinate's behavior. Leaders are obligated to show subordinates what behavior is expected, and punishment can show them only what is *not* expected. But when a subordinate clearly knows, but refuses to comply, leaders may need to punish.

Before imposing punishment, leaders should consider outside counseling as a first response to subordinates whose infractions at work are the result of outside problems, as for example with substance abuse, marital conflict, or mismanagement of personal finances.

In a West Point leadership course, instructors offer cadets research psychologist Douglas MacGregor's metaphor of touching a hot stove to teach simple, effective punishment: the stove is swift in its message, relatively intense, impersonal (does not lose its temper), singles out precisely the errant behavior, consistent (the result is always the same), and offers an alternative behavior. Employed within these guidelines, the following forms of punishment can be effective:

✳ *Verbal chastisement.* After a discussion of the facts of the situation with the subordinate—to make sure that the leader's understanding is valid—a verbal reprimand is a good first-level response. It should reinforce the expected behavior and the understanding that the person's behavior—not the person himself—is the problem.

The point is to correct behavior, and not to humiliate. This may require a great deal of self-control on the part of the leader who, no matter how angry, must control his temper. With some chagrin, I remember an experience I had in Vietnam in which I failed to fulfill the principles of responsible role-modeling and two-way communication. Morale was low in my company. As I mentioned earlier, we were under pressure to finish building an airfield, everyone was tired, demoralized, and stressed out. Walking by a dump truck, I saw two malingerers sleeping in its hauling bed. Fatigued myself, I chewed them out—with a ferocity that reminded me, in retrospect, of the most abusive upperclassmen I had known at West Point.

What I remember most of all is the look of frightened disappointment that crossed their faces. Immediately I thought to myself: "You have no right to talk to people that way. And they know you have no right." When I finished, they shrunk away. I was ashamed. I knew my behavior had been a mistake and I learned from it—I never again yelled at a soldier.

✳ *Firing.* As a first-incident response, on-the-spot firing is justified only in the face of incontrovertible evidence of moral turpitude or flawed character. Otherwise, it is justified after all reasonable efforts to provide guidance, counseling, and reprimands have been to no avail. Douglas MacArthur asked of himself as a leader, "Do I use moral courage in getting rid of subordinates who have proven themselves beyond doubt to be unfit?"

PRIVACY

Douglas MacArthur also said, "Praise in public, admonish in private." This maxim reflects the importance of respecting the dignity of the subordinate. After all, the goal is correction, not humiliation. It's the leader's responsibility to protect the esteem of his direct reports in the eyes of their direct reports.

One of the saddest memories of my Army career came in Korea when my superior chose to punish me for an unintentional omission by humiliating me in front of five peers and subordinates. My anger with his leadership failure was much stronger than my attention to my own failure.

A LONG WAY FROM ZERO

In the beginning of this book I described R-Day and its followership lessons from the viewpoint of entering plebes. Now at this pass, let's look at R-Day from a different point of view—that of the squad leaders who, during their third summer, are the upperclass cadets in charge of making sure that all the events of this very busy day run like clockwork.

The young leaders now become the cadets in the red sashes whom they admired so much when they were newborn plebes. By the time they reach their third year, many cadets have forgotten how far they have come so quickly. All the commands and skills and rituals that seemed so bewildering to them as plebes are now as obvious as coming in out of the rain. When they come face to face with the plebes they are about to initiate into the ways of West Point, a strange thing happens. A new plebe will ask a question—something like, "Sir, is there a correct way to tie my shoes?" The upperclass cadet is dumbstruck, realizing these plebes know nothing—absolutely nothing.

Soon the squad leaders realize that when they look at these plebes they are looking at themselves in a mirror, only two years earlier. While they are astonished at the plebes' ignorance, they are just as astonished to realize that they themselves were equally ignorant two years ago. They've come a long way from zero.

This is one of the most important lessons of leadership taught at West Point: No one gets anywhere alone. These well-turned-out and competent juniors in red sashes owe their success, in large part, to all the leaders-in-training who helped them along. And now it is time for them to reach out a hand to their younger colleagues.

You can almost see this realization in the faces of the cadets. It inspires me over and over again to see them make this leap of understanding. They are taking on the full responsibility of leadership with great personal pride and dignity. A cadet who may have been less than diligent for two entire years about shining his shoes, polishing his belt buckle, and keeping his uniform clean and pressed will now do so conscientiously—because he is responsible for eight plebes who are looking at him as their example of a good cadet. The upperclass cadet remembers the sense of awe he first felt for his own squad leader, and now wants to inspire the same in his group of plebes.

It is hard work. Squad leaders get much less sleep than the plebes they're in charge of. They wake up earlier and go to bed later. One West Pointer recalls, "I worked harder as a squad leader in Beast than I did when I was a plebe in Beast. As a plebe I was exhausted by the pace of activity but also from the fear that I'd get in trouble. As an upperclassman I had a lot of late nights and I went through a lot of shoe polish. I was exhausted because I cared so much."

THIRD PASS:

Acquiring the Self-Reliance

to Lead Leaders

9

Pushing Character to an Extreme

At a recent panel discussion at an Ivy League university, a hypothetical situation was proposed by Jack Welch, the chairman of General Electric, to the audience. You are representing a U.S. company in a South American dictatorship, he said, and about to close a deal that would represent $90 million to the company. Your counterpart in the arrangement assures you that the deal looks very good; that the contract is close to being signed. The only loose end is a matter of depositing $1 million in a certain Swiss bank account.

"How many of you would make the deposit?" Welch asked the audience.

About a third of the students raised their hands, which left him momentarily speechless.

Finally, he said, "They're not teaching you everything you need to know here."

Third Pass

In the Second Pass of leadership training the cadets raise their sights from toeing the line to entertaining the possibility that the organization might make a bad decision. The Third Pass of leadership training forces the cadets to think in realistic detail about what they would actually *do* in a morally complex situation.

What the Academy teaches them to do in such a situation is to go to extremes in matters of principle. One must become comfortable risking everything—one's career, one's life—to keep principles alive. Leadership requires this kind of commitment on a daily basis, not just when one is in a crisis.

I am, for example, convinced that the public good and my private integrity are more important than profits, promotions, or career. When I was a twenty-two-year-old lieutenant on my first assignment in the Army, a senior general officer gave some sound and blunt advice to a group of young officers. He told us, "Be prepared to give up your career tomorrow."

He suggested we make up our minds in advance that our integrity was more important than our careers—and that no situation should convince us to compromise that integrity. Once we had made up our minds, no boss would be able to bully us into a breech of integrity.

I liked his advice and have tried to follow it. This has not always been easy. I once worked for a commander whose decisions I had so little respect for that I couldn't help but disagree with him—frequently and vociferously. Indeed, when I finished my tour of duty and later stopped by the personnel office in Washington, I was so sure I'd have to look for a new job that I said to the personnel officer something along the lines of, "I assume my career's over." To my surprise, my commander must have respected my disagreements because his evaluation of me was strongly positive.

No matter how much I have invested in a career, I would hope to have the courage to walk away from it rather than violate my integrity. There are always other jobs, other careers.

At age seventy-five, when I am on the porch in my rocking chair, I don't want to have to admit to myself, "I compromised myself to get ahead or grow rich." I don't want to have regrets. This perspective has often helped me in the face of temptation.

One of the most astonishingly extreme examples of defending one's integrity happened during the Vietnam war. Admiral James B. Stockdale was forced to bail out of his plane over North Vietnam, knowing as he did so that he was most likely destined to become a prisoner of war. In the great drama of life, Stockdale had never wanted to play the role of POW. However, the role was assigned to him, and he decided to play it to the best of his ability. At one point he knew that, if tortured further, he might well be forced to divulge information that would betray his countrymen. So, in order to outwit his captors, he beat himself unconscious with a stool in his cell.

Stockdale is an example of commitment to principles—above career, above even life.

WHEN TO BREAK GOOD RULES

As illustrated in a previous chapter, the cadets' moral education begins with moral rules—"a cadet does not lie, cheat, steal, nor tolerate those who do." West Point believes in these rules and in the superiority of a community governed by a moral code.

But the world is not always so simple. It is rendered in shades of gray, not black and white, and our young leaders must learn to make decisions in situations that present complicated, sometimes heart-rending, moral conflicts. Often this means violating one rule in order to keep another—because it makes moral sense to do so. In their junior year, in a series of honor and moral philosophy classes, the Academy uses case studies and role-playing to prepare cadets to face such conflicts.

In one class, the teacher proposes a hypothetical but realistic situation:

> *The time is World War II. You are a Dutch trawler captain transporting Jewish children "underground" to safety. A German Navy patrol boat stops your ship and the Germans demand to know what cargo you're carrying. You sense that if you lie, you may be allowed to pass unmolested. But if you tell the truth you will surely forfeit the children's lives—and probably your own. What do you do?*

An adult civilian would not likely have a great moral struggle over lying in this situation. But not lying is one of the four inviolate absolutes that the nineteen- and twenty-year-old cadets have been living with for the past two years. Indeed, this may be the first time in their lives that they have thought about whether it would ever be morally justifiable to lie. Some will volunteer this reaction:

"Sir, I will tell the truth!"

"Why?"

"Because I will not lie, cheat, steal, or tolerate those who do!"

Their commitment to truth and absolute rules has been reinforced by their having recently studied Kant's "categorical imperative," presented in examples posed by the philosopher in which lying would be unacceptable even in life-or-death situations.

By questioning, the instructor encourages cadets to recognize the conflicting moral obligations confronted by the trawler captain—truth-telling versus protecting innocent lives. The instructor also suggests as a viewpoint that the German Navy is acting outside the moral sphere to such an extent that the Germans forfeit the right to expect the truth. Most cadets, not without some anguish, eventually conclude that the trawler captain is right to lie. They are usually comfortable with the utilitarian reasoning, as proposed by Jeremy Bentham and John Stuart Mill, which supports this conclusion. However, the utilitarian argument is soon shown to have limitations by the next hypothetical situation posed.

The teacher lines up five cadets along the blackboard. Each represents a villager in a small country in the midst of a civil war. They are about to be executed by a firing squad, represented by five other cadets lined up against the opposite wall. The sergeant in charge (played by the instructor) announces that four of the villagers will be allowed to live—if a foreigner who stumbles upon the scene (another cadet) shoots *one* of the five villagers. The sergeant places a rifle in the hands of the cadet role-playing the foreign visitor, and tells her to shoot. What should she do?

Sometimes, this class evokes more animated student participation than any other. The utilitarian argument is frequently evoked: "Sir, I would kill one person to save four other lives!"

"I would try to kill the officer instead!"

"But that will get you killed!"

Some, however, come to the conclusion that they would refuse to become a killer even to save lives. They will conclude that the sergeant's immorality must not be a vehicle to make them immoral also.

In the two above examples, I believe the choices that exhibit the most character are (1) lying to the German patrol boat, and (2) refusing to kill a villager. But these are merely my choices, and they are not the point of the class. The point is that *in the complexities of life, perfectly sound moral rules, on their face, can come into conflict with one another.* Most real-life decisions aren't as dramatic as our hypothetical cases, but the class sensitizes the cadets to the need to be able to reason through profound and enigmatically difficult situations.

Maintaining personal and organizational integrity requires constant self-vigilance on the part of the leader. Due to the fast pace of business, or for the sake of convenience, it is very easy to lose sensitivity to moral issues. We develop moral calluses, so to speak, and call it "being professional." However, once we have acted without regard to moral implications, even in a minuscule matter—for example, signing a contract to pay a supplier in thirty days when we consciously have no intention to pay for sixty or ninety—it becomes that much easier for lax moral behavior to become a pattern, even in more important issues.

For most of his book *Just and Unjust Wars*, Michael Walzer argues in favor of a moral structure in which even wars should be constrained. He argues persuasively that armies should function within the rules of war, according to international law and the Geneva Conventions. However, in his final chapters, Walzer veers from this position and switches to an ultimately utilitarian argument. He suggests that in a supreme emergency—say, if Hitler were about to win World War II—and if civilization as we know it were threatened with extinction, then and only then would it be justified to abandon the rules of war to win the war.

Of course, in your business or in mine now, we are not very likely ever to encounter a situation that endangers civilization as we know it. Perhaps that means that you and I should never abandon our moral structure. It almost certainly means we should pay our bills on time when we've promised to do so.

A leader can't just go along with the crowd. On the contrary, a leader must stand alone, deliver unpleasant news, be the one to say, "This is not working out, let's fix it." There is no leadership without judgment. As we have seen, classroom exercises help cadets fine-tune their decision-making apparatus

—hitting them with hard moral dilemmas that increase their self-awareness and self-reliance. When the cadets rise to the next level of leadership—indirect leadership in which they learn to lead other leaders—they find themselves standing alone more and more frequently.

10

Leading Leaders

F ollowership taught cadets how to relate to superiors. The honor code taught them peer conduct. Face-to-face leadership taught them to care deeply about both their immediate goal and the people who must accomplish it.

Now in the cadet's third year, placed in an *indirect* leadership role for the first time, the young leader raises his focus from dealing directly with the people who accomplish the goals to dealing with their leaders.

By the time he reaches this pass of training, the cadet excels at fixing problems. The demands of indirect leadership, however, are such that he must now learn to resist this impulse in the service of learning a newer and bigger skill: orchestrating the activities of a more complex group of individuals to accomplish a greater given task. Surprisingly few managers appreciate the kind of sophisticated communication necessary for getting the job done. Peter Senge says that managers don't take management seriously. "They always want to fix things, not create systems that eliminate problems." Cadets get their first taste of serious management after a year spent practicing face-to-face leadership, when they are promoted to "middle management." As squad leaders they are responsible for the performance of the entire squad (not just one or two plebes)—an exponential growth in responsibility.

As a leader moves upward in the hierarchy from direct leadership to indirect—and beyond—she moves progressively away from direct interaction with followers. She moves toward broadened responsibility, helping other leaders solve the problems that they have identified.

CONSERVING YOUR ENERGY AS A LEADER

The success of the indirect leader depends in part on his ability to delegate responsibility to his subordinate leaders. An indirect leader who doesn't delegate spends so much time putting out brushfires that he has no time to look after the larger interests of the group.

People resist delegating for various reasons. Some are concerned that the job won't be performed correctly if they leave it to someone else. Others feel personally reduced when they share power. Still others complain that training a subordinate leader is just too time-consuming when they could be doing the job themselves.

While training a subordinate *is* time-consuming, it is time well spent. It ultimately frees the leader to think about larger issues.

A squad leader must learn instead to raise her focus. If she notices a plebe committing an error, instead of issuing direct orders to correct it, she must instead ask herself, "How can I help my team leader—my direct subordinate—to improve this plebe's performance?" Usually, the answer to this question is straightforward. For example, one squad leader I know had noticed a plebe in her squad who was performing poorly. Too often, his shoes were ill-shined at the noon formation, and he had received an unusually high number of demerits for failing to keep his room neat and orderly. After watching for some days to see if the team leader would correct the situation, the squad leader finally chose to speak to the team leader about the plebe's substandard performance.

When she asked if the team leader was aware of the plebe's problems, the team leader said that not only was he aware of them, but that there were still more problems that the squad leader didn't know about. The plebe was also shirking his share of team duties, such as delivering laundry and carrying mail. The team leader added that he was growing exasperated at the plebe's failure to respond to his corrections.

So the squad leader asked the team leader how thoroughly he had discussed the problem with the plebe.

The team leader admitted that they hadn't discussed it at all—he had merely chastised the plebe verbally a couple of times, with no visible effect. The squad leader then role-played such a discussion with the team leader, reminding him that the goal was to discover *why* the plebe was not functioning well.

When the team leader talked with the plebe, he found that he was from a very small town, a graduate of a modest high school. He was desperately afraid of flunking out of West Point and being sent home "in shame." Therefore, he was spending every possible moment in the library studying instead of attending to his plebe duties. This discussion enabled the team leader to arrange for tutors for the plebe. He gave him permission to spend an extra afternoon each week studying—insisting that the plebe pitch in with his share of duties. With this encouragement, the plebe was happy—and able—to do so.

Instead of intervening personally with the troubled plebe, the squad leader pointed her team leader in the right direction—making sure he had the tools necessary to solve the problem. This paid off for everyone: the plebe got help with what was really bothering him, the team leader learned a valuable technique of leadership, and the squad leader solved a serious problem with a minimum investment of her own time.

KNOWING WHAT'S IMPORTANT

Early in my military career, I served as aide-de-camp for General Willard Roper, who supervised the engineer brigade working throughout the northern half of Vietnam. Among his staff's duties was a need to answer important letters of inquiry from members of Congress regarding complaints from soldiers and constituents. Roper would read the letters his staff had written to ensure that they had answered the congressional query thoroughly. If he found that they contained the necessary information, albeit with minor grammatical or typographical errors, he would sign them and send them on to Washington without having them retyped. He recognized that one of life's realities is that we cannot do everything. We must use our limited resources as best we can to accomplish what we believe to be most important. As Teddy Roosevelt put it, "Do what you can, with what you have, where you are."

THE LEADER WHO DOES NOT DELEGATE IS NOT TRULY LEADING

I discovered early in my tour in Vietnam that Rick Gorski, a West Point classmate of mine, served as aide-de-camp to the general who was General Roper's counterpart in the southern half of the country. (I will call him General X.) Whenever the two generals had meetings with top brass in Saigon headquarters, Gorski and I would compare notes.

General Roper was a superb delegator. He selected his key subordinates very carefully and then gave them wide latitude in which to work. "Just bring me the problems you cannot solve," was his charge to us. This left Roper with so much spare time that one of my biggest challenges was to keep him stocked with library books to occupy his idle evening hours.

General X, on the other hand, had no time for library books. He had to see every single sheet of paper that came into or went out of his headquarters, and he personally supervised every urgent action. He worked every waking moment. One of Gorski's biggest challenges was to balance two brief-cases full of papers so that General X could work on them while being transported from one headquarters to another.

The purpose of delegation is not solely to make time for a leader to read library books. What most impressed me was that the free time General Roper generated for himself through delegation enabled him to keep his focus raised and see the big organizational picture. For instance, he had enough foresight to begin a year and a half in advance the bureaucratic process of ordering a multimillion-dollar pur-chase of the construction equipment that he knew would be sorely needed by then. By contrast, General X was so mired in minutia that, when questioned, he had no idea what equipment he would need a year and a half down the line, and could only make vague promises to look into the matter.

Only Roper was truly fulfilling his role as a leader.

With each promotion, an indirect leader must constantly raise her focus, alter her paradigm, enlarge her frame of refer-ence, and not get caught in the trap of simply doing her previous job under the auspices of a more lofty title. There are several techniques she can use to ensure that her focus re-mains raised.

＊ *Constant self-examination.* An indirect leader should take time to consider the important elements of his perfor-mance. Among the questions he should ask himself: Am I practicing self-restraint? Do I have the guts to sit back and delegate? Do I get too involved in minor details? Do I try to do my subordinates' work for them?

✳ *Develop immediate subordinates.* Think through each subordinate's role with him, and find ways to mentor him toward success. This is what General Roper did. He chose high-quality people, made sure they clearly understood their responsibilities, were well trained—and then set them free to do their jobs without his constant involvement. Thus he could keep his own vision raised.

✳ *Engage in strategic thinking.* Figure out what your department should be doing a year—or several years—down the line. Begin working toward those goals early. Dave Palmer, for example, maintained a strategic focus while governing West Point, always thinking of the Academy's role in meeting the Army's and the nation's future need for military leaders.

STYLES OF DELEGATION

Each leader develops his own style of delegation. Dave Palmer delegated in the style of an orchestral conductor—visibly coordinating the actions of his team members, signaling each staffer and subordinate leader on what he should be doing and when. During the late 1980s, each of his key subordinates managed a different project. My domain was to facilitate the strategic planning process, an umbrella over many studies of the Academy's programs.

By knowing in detail what each of his key subordinates was doing, Palmer deftly made sure the projects hung together in a unified manner. He was so involved in these details that he effectively became his own chief coordinator and integrator (a job which most senior Army leaders delegate to a chief of staff).

I think he was able to handle as much as he did because of his extraordinary capacity to manage both details and the big picture simultaneously. He worked long hours, was a rapid reader with high comprehension, could work through mountains of paperwork at night and maintain a high volume of interactions with subordinates and outsiders during the day. Things worked extremely smoothly under his leadership because he knew more than anyone else about *all* of the key staffers' areas.

In contrast, General Roper, as I've mentioned, delegated more details to capable subordinates—including a chief of staff—than Palmer did, and left managing the big picture for himself.

This allowed him a more tolerable workload than Palmer, but still enabled him to be a highly successful leader—because he kept his eye to the horizon, his ear to the ground, and his hand on the helm. Therefore, I'd compare him to a theatrical director—one who is not visible to the audience but has, behind the scenes, been directly in charge of the way the action proceeds.

One man conducted, the other directed. Both delegated, requiring subordinates to perform, although their styles of doing so were different. Most significantly, both were successful leaders because both kept the big picture in focus.

MAN IN THE MIDDLE

An indirect leader must be loyal to those *above* him and those *below* him simultaneously—to the group he heads (for cadets, the squad; for corporate managers, the department) and to the larger group his unit belongs to (at West Point, the cadet platoon; in business, the division). Bringing these loyalties into alignment is one of the challenges of indirect leadership.

I remember a top cadet officer standing before his class at the beginning of the academic year saying that he was going to have to enforce an unpopular policy—mandatory "lights out" at midnight—because the Commandant had insisted upon it.

Later, it was pointed out that blaming the policy on his leader was an act of disloyalty. Indeed, it exemplified poor followership.

It is the duty and responsibility of an indirect leader who disagrees with a policy to privately voice his objections and doubts about the policy to his leader. However, if his leader refuses to change the policy, then he should publicly support the final decision and make every effort to ensure the success of the leader's decision.

REFUSE WET BABIES

Sometimes, as we have seen, indirect leaders fail to delegate. But sometimes indirect leaders fail because their subordinates are afraid to make the decisions their leader has delegated to them. Instead, they try to fob off their decision-making responsibilities on their bosses.

In the U.S. State Department they call this syndrome "leaving their wet babies on our doorstep." Many ambassadors have had the experience of opening the embassy doors in the morning to find a crying baby on the doorstep—so new to the world that it was still wet. The baby, who should have been his mother's problem, has just become the ambassador's.

Leaders who allow—or even encourage—their subordinates to give them wet babies are in for a rough ride. Their dilemma is identical to that of the leader who fails to delegate: They have left themselves no time to do their actual job, which is to look out for the larger good of the group.

The first thing a leader who finds himself in this position must do is gently hand the baby back to the parent. As I entered my new job as college president, I found that several of my subordinates had acquired the habit of bringing all of their problems to the president for resolution. At first they looked at me with disappointment when I deflected them and sent them out the door with their problems remaining on their own shoulders. I was happy to discuss, and suggest, and engage in problem analysis with them—but I was not willing to accept responsibility for solving their problems.

Before long, they began exercising their renewed authority without my insistence. The price I paid was that, occasionally, their solutions were not the ones I would have chosen. But this was an economical, necessary price to acquire a synergistic team willing and able to act with interdependence.

And developing such a team is precisely the goal of indirect leadership. Just as the indirect leader has moved away from the production floor by delegating his previous responsibilities, and has raised his vision to encompass a broadened scope of responsibilities, so, as he enters executive levels, will he encounter similar, but more extreme changes in the type of leadership that is needed. That is executive leadership and is described in the following chapter.

FOURTH PASS:

Serving as the Organization's
Eyes and Ears

11

Executive Leadership

Executive leaders have two questions uppermost in their minds: Who are we? And where are we going—today, tomorrow, and into the next decade? If the executive leaders are not thinking "big picture" and "long term"—and not just five years, but twenty-five years—then no one else in the organization will be able to look far into the future either. They must become, in essence, the eyes and ears of the organization, seeing, thinking, sensing, rather than actually *doing*. The executive leader is similar to the highest stage of leadership which Mayan leaders called "echo man"—a leader who picks up signals and sends them out.* This leader at the pinnacle has as his or her most important role not direct action, but symbolism—inspiring people in the di-

---

* Robert Bly, *What the Mayans Could Teach the Joint Chiefs, New York Times,* July 23, 1993, p. A27.

rection of the bigger picture. The executive leader communicates this purpose to large numbers of people—many of whom he or she may never meet or talk with—through a complex web of both staff and subordinate leaders. Rather than using direct, interpersonal discussion, the executive leaders influence subordinates primarily by indirect communication and policy decisions.

The Academy gives senior cadets a taste of executive leadership during their fourth year. The Academy does not spend as much time on this level of leadership as it does on the others because these lessons will not be relevant to the cadets for many years. Most leaders do not practice executive leadership until well along in their careers.

The four-thousand-strong Corps of Cadets is organized into a military brigade, which is divided into four regiments. Each regiment is divided into three battalions, each battalion into three companies, each company into three or four platoons, each platoon into three or four squads, and each squad into two or three teams. In previous chapters we have examined the leadership of the smallest functional units—the team and the squad, by direct and indirect leaders respectively. Every unit above these has an organizational, or executive, leader.

In the first chapter, I summarized the four passes of leadership in West Point's program. In a military parade performed by cadets on the Plain we see all the levels of leadership working together simultaneously. The plebe's, or follower's, job is to be dressed correctly, at the ceremony on time, in step with the beat of the drum, rifle held at the proper angle. The team (direct) leaders have the same responsibilities, in addition to which, during the parade, they coach the team

("Smith, increase your arm swing"). Squad—indirect—leaders make sure their squads know in advance what uniform to wear, when to show up, and have practiced every move to perfection. The executive leaders—cadet officers—have planned and organized the entire event, including rehearsing the Corps and afterward evaluating the whole performance.

The challenge the senior cadets face, for which West Point trains them, is to look away from the team and themselves and to see the organization as a whole as their first responsibility.

A BRIDGE BETWEEN THE INSIDE AND THE OUTSIDE

Just as all leaders serve as the bridge between those *below* them and those *above* them, the organizational leaders at the highest level are the bridge between those *inside* the organization and the *outside* world.

Every organization lives within a broad, sustaining social context—its environment, in which it provides society's members something of value and receives in return what it needs to thrive.

A business supplies useful products or services and receives the wherewithal—labor, raw materials, capital goods—it needs from the outside. In turn, people outside the organization receive from the business its products, a source of employment, and tax support of their government. Government involves the business through laws in its social agenda. In this interdependent, ever-shifting relationship of the organization and its environment, the executive leader is the focal point of the exchange process, accomplishing the practical goals of representing the organization and negotiating on its behalf as well as the larger goal of continually reimagining what the organization is and what it can be in the future.

To successfully accomplish their role as a conduit inside and outside of the organization, executive leaders must work for the greater good of both, effectively spanning the gap between the organization and the community, guided by the constraints each imposes. In a sense, the principal task of an executive leader is to find a way in which, to paraphrase an old business saying, "What is good for the community is good for the organization"—and vice versa.

For example, I illustrated in an earlier chapter how, in my position as president of the College of the Albemarle, I determined that the community's need for a nearby, historically black college to serve all people of our region of North Carolina was more important than the immediate needs of my college. In other words, I decided that, in that particular instance, we *inside* the organization would accommodate the *outside*. On the other hand, there are times when I find that the opposite is the case—that the immediate, inside needs of my college are so important that outside constraints should be altered if possible.

For example, one of the key resources my college acquires from the outside world is funding of our facilities' maintenance and repair by local county government. One spring I found that my budget had not been approved by the finance committee of the Board of County Commissioners, who intended to allot us less money than I thought we needed. However, I believed we were already too constrained by previous budget cuts, so I went back to them with further explanations of my circumstances and asked for reconsideration of my budget. They agreed with my analysis, and provided most of the increase which we needed. This was an instance where I felt it would serve the greater good more for the accommodation to come from outside my organization, and not inside.

EVEN EXECUTIVE LEADERS ARE STILL FOLLOWERS

Executives have substantial power, but still must function within boundaries. It is easy to forget that, despite being the highest leaders in their organizations, they are still followers. If they don't have a direct boss, they have to report to some kind of leader—be it the board, the clients, or the shareholders.

This, the first lesson I learned at West Point, comes back to me time and time again. I remember one Brigade Commander (the highest-ranking cadet officer) who forgot this irreducible truth. He was absolutely convinced that the Corps was well prepared for a parade and didn't require the final scheduled rehearsal. Insistently, he tried to convince his boss, the Commandant, to let him cancel the practice. The Commandant was not convinced, but the cadet commander wouldn't take no for an answer.

Finally, exasperated, the Commandant stood up and said, "Mr. Smith, I want you to stand at attention, feet together, hands at your side, eyes straight ahead, mouth closed! Mr. Smith, listen to me: We are not going to cancel parade practice on Friday. I say again, we are not going to cancel the parade practice. Do you understand?" This was a powerful—

and embarrassing—reminder that the lessons of followership can never be forgotten.

CARRY A BIG SIGN

The primary leadership responsibility of all executive leaders inside their organizations is to continually inspire their members to move toward the larger goals of the institution. Executive leaders should use every opportunity to reinforce the institution's identity and purpose. Every single interaction can be used to remind people of the organization's mission.

During his years as the executive leader of West Point, from 1986 to 1992, General Dave Palmer excelled at both communication and symbolism. In fact, he was so unrelenting in pointing people of the institution back to the overarching purpose and their role in it that it was almost as if he walked around every day carrying a big sign overhead saying, "Don't forget the purpose of the United States Military Academy is to provide the nation with leaders of character who serve the common defense—and what you are doing here and now contributes to that noble cause [or if it doesn't, let's change it to make sure it does]."

FUNCTIONS OF THE EXECUTIVE LEADER

There are a few functions that define the essence of executive leadership. Executive leaders would do well to master each of them.

✷ *Integration.* The executive leader is like an orchestra conductor or theatrical director, responsible for making all the departments within the organization work harmoniously together as one unit. For example, as a college president, I have three key subordinates—one in charge of classroom instruction, another of all student processing and outside-of-classroom activities, and a third of support services (food, budget, building maintenance). Many of the decisions of one affect the others. Whenever the large decisions within one or more divisions have to be made, I bring my subordinates together as a team for problem-solving sessions. We thus can iron out the ways in which each of their divisions is affected. The efficiency of operation and the quality of service to our clients would be severely diminished if I permitted them to make major decisions regarding their own divisions in isolation from the others.

✷ *Coordination.* Coordination is similar to but not identical with integration. It involves contacting all those whose action is needed to fulfill a task, or all those who will be affected by a potential decision—to gain their perspectives on the impact of a decision before it is made, or to ensure they are prepared to do their part when needed. For example, before a major event, such as a graduation ceremony, I get all the important participants together in one room to go through the sequence of events to be sure everyone knows their part.

✴ *Assimilation of details.* To the outside observer, an executive's day looks so fragmented, fractured, frenetic, and filled with brief interactions that their ability to lead under such circumstances may seem inexplicable. Yet the best executive leaders are capable of managing myriad details—mining the ore from many small interactions while keeping their eye on the big picture.

In my present job I collect bits of data from each conversation regarding dozens of subjects. Sometimes, I will later recall something a faculty member told me earlier, because it suddenly illuminates an issue that is before me at the moment. For example, in a group session with my staff, discussing remote learning opportunities, I recalled another staff member showing me some now-dormant TV broadcasting equipment which could be used for televised course work. That led other staff members to mention still other TV resources available to us.

As another example, I learned from my dean of students that Gladys Whitehurst, our head custodian, is one of our best sources of information about students (who the potential troublemakers are, for example). As she is constantly moving through the hallways, she sees students interacting all day long. However, since they do not perceive her as an authority figure, they do not alter their behavior when she's around. Thus, she becomes a unique and invaluable source of useful information about students for the senior leaders of the college. We as the leaders, however, in order to gain that information, must first recognize her value and second take the time to chat with her occasionally. In the same way as Gladys, every member of the organization has a unique perspective which can be of value to leaders.

❋ *Seeing the big picture.* An executive leader can become *too* detail-oriented, and must make sure to balance these interactions with a constant eye on the big picture. Dave Palmer was, in my experience, unmatched at simultaneously managing a high volume of details and keeping his focus on the large organization. He might be studying a detailed schedule of the construction of a new visitors' center at West Point, and in the next breath he could sit back and explain how that facility played a role in the Academy's purpose of developing leaders of character: say, imbuing a sense of pride in and appreciation for the cadets among visitors, and, in turn, a sense of responsibility in the cadets to fulfill the visitors' image of them.

❋ *Ability to recognize a multiplicity of perspectives, and assimilate all of them.* Just as Gladys, the head custodian, offers me a unique and valuable perspective, I recognize that having access to many and differing perspectives is likely to bring me as close to reality or objective truth as I can get.

I had a friend who was a criminal investigator, who told me that a maxim of his trade is to beware when all of the "eyewitness reports" from a crime or accident scene match up identically. That, he says, is a sure sign of collusion. Instead, most such reports will have conflicting elements representing separate pieces of a puzzle which he as investigator must resolve.

Likewise, the leaders who mine ore from many small interactions must put the varying stories together to discover a useful truth for their organizations, much the way a detective solves a crime. Moreover, if the leader is *not* getting conflicting stories or opinions, it should be a danger signal. As General Patton used to say, "If everyone is thinking alike, no one is thinking." The story is told that Alfred Sloan, the leader of General Motors from 1923 to 1946, refused to make a decision which was unanimously supported by his subordinates. He reasoned, "If we don't know more reasons not to do this than we know now, we probably don't know enough about it, period. Let's wait ninety days." They did, and within ninety days they had discovered the faults of the proposed decision.

✳ *Diplomacy*. True diplomacy arises when an executive leader is possessed of a touch of humility regarding his own grasp of relevant information, and genuine acceptance of multiple perspectives. With this humility, he can sincerely respect the value of contrary opinions and honestly thank someone who has the courage to disagree and let her know that her contribution is valued. At my college, after telling the faculty in a meeting that I would not read anonymous notes, a faculty member approached me afterward to object. He pointed out that from my position of power, I could not expect people to give me negative—but necessary—feedback on my own leadership face to face. Although I had adopted the policy against anonymous notes to protect faculty members from accusations against them by others, I hadn't considered accusations against myself. We were both right about anonymous notes—but looking at them from different perspectives. I went back to the faculty, publicly thanked the member who disagreed with me, and announced a revision to my policy. I now accept anonymous notes that are critical of me, but not of others.

✳ *Well-versed in one's business.* Even at the top of organizations, the highest-performing executive leaders still have high levels of task competence in their chosen fields. Business literature constantly evokes case histories of companies trying to diversify by taking over healthy companies in industries they were not familiar with. Because they did not "know their business," their takeover strategies were dismal failures. There are also positive examples of the power of knowing one's business—Rupert Murdoch instructing his pressmen on how to use their equipment to convert a broadsheet to a tabloid; Disney executive Marty Kaplan putting himself through a self-designed university to learn every aspect of the movie business. In my case—and in the case of thousands of soldiers —knowing my business saved lives.

When I became a college president, I did not assume that I knew all I needed to know about it, despite many of my years in the military being in education. I sought out other college presidents in the region—for their counsel, which has been invaluable to me—especially on local political matters. For example, my very first mentor was a woman who heads a community college in South Carolina, who visited my college and gave me immensely useful advice on how to get started. For example, she told me that on her first day on the job, she took her senior staff on a tour of the entire campus so that they would be seen together, and perceived, as a team. I did the same thing.

A leader's primary responsibility is to the organization he leads, not to his own career or ambition. Executive leaders should pay particular attention to succession planning. I recently hired a new dean of students—my second in command at the college. Among the questions I asked the candidates during the interview process was whether they imagined themselves assuming my job, or another presidency, a few years down the line. Some were taken aback by this question, but the one I chose was not—she told me without hesitation that it was her goal to be a president within a few years. Effective leaders want the best, most competent people around them—and are not threatened by them.

Executive leadership is a state of constant learning. There can be no sitting back, no relaxing. Executive leaders are at the pinnacle of management but they will stay there only if they keep evolving. Indeed, leadership development is a process that never finishes. To paraphrase retailer E. A. Filene, "When a person's development as a leader is finished, that leader is finished."

OUT IN THE WORLD:

From Learning Principled

Leadership to Practicing It

12

Following Our Own Advice

The autocratic factory foreman who tries to bully his line personnel into production; the middle manager who treats his underlings with a snide manner; the shop steward who browbeats in a domineering tone of voice; the executive who treats subordinates superciliously—they all are subject to the same problems the abusive cadet suffered in earlier eras at West Point. All too frequently civilian leaders, as well as military ones, seem to think that subordinates must be driven like animals to get them to produce—to obey. And that their leadership positions somehow exempt them from humane, considerate treatment of their subordinates. But impatience, mistrust, contempt, and lack of communication can evoke only disharmony and low productivity. Unreasonably high stress can only provoke further organizational problems.

Maintaining productive relationships between leaders and subordinates is *not* a uniquely West Point, or military, issue.

Indeed, when you peruse West Point's dimensions of leadership and principles of leader-subordinate relationships, which follow at the end of this chapter, you will find that only a fraction of them pertain to a military context. And in those few items, if you substitute the name of your organization for that of West Point, you'll find that the principle applies and will be useful to you also.

Those principles were conceived at West Point as part of efforts to reform the Academy's historic "plebe system," and the story of those reforms offers many helpful insights to practicing leaders.

Throughout much of West Point's history, several questionable practices—such as hazing, harassment, screaming, and cruel, terrorizing jokes—were traditional behavior by the upper three classes of cadets toward plebes. Despite many attempts during the nineteenth and twentieth centuries to temper or end these practices, it was not until the 1980s and 1990s that much progress was made—and that because only then was it officially recognized that a West Point education was a complicated, four-year process of leadership development, and not just a system of strengthening the character of plebes.

The long period it took to effect these changes illustrates the difficulties that leaders face when attempting to change undesirable elements within the entrenched culture of a mature organization.

The plebe system became known formally as the "Fourth Class System" when Douglas MacArthur, as West Point Superintendent in the 1920s, attempted to reform it. This very name indicates that cadets were divided into two groups—plebes, or fourth-class cadets, and everyone else. Most frequently, the hazing of the plebes stayed within reasonable if unpleasant limits. Unfortunately, the threshold of rationality was occasionally crossed.

For instance, at the turn of the century, according to historians Scott Dillard and Roger Nye, a plebe named Booz got into trouble because he was incorrectly instructed on his guard duties. When he was corrected by some upperclassmen, he refused to change because he believed he must explicitly obey the instructions—however faulty—of the corporal of the guard. The infuriated upperclassmen challenged him to fight a representative of their class, who beat him badly.

To make matters worse, word spread among the upperclassmen that Booz had given up the fight intentionally, to avoid an even worse beating. He was forced to consume hot sauce in the dining hall—a whole bottle within a week. In September 1898, he resigned and returned home. About two years later he died of an ailment vaguely described as "tuberculosis of the throat." Whether the death was attributable to his treatment at West Point is not clear.

Harsh discipline in the military has a rational historical context. Before West Point was established in 1802, many armies were composed of uneducated, mercenary elements of society who capitalized on their best—if not their only—opportunity for a legitimate income. These men were unruly, exploitative, and frequently uncivilized. Hence the traditions of harsh treatment; as Douglas MacArthur said, these soldiers required "the most rigid methods of training, the severest forms of discipline."

However, such traditions of discipline lived on long after the need for them had passed. Indeed, efforts to reform the plebe system had begun some twenty years before the Booz incident. In the decade after the Civil War, hazing practices at the Academy took a sharp turn for the worse. By 1879, Superintendent John Schofield was moved to make an impassioned speech before the cadets, saying:

> The practice of hazing has not at West Point even the poor excuse that is urged for it at civil colleges. For the military discipline and instruction which all new cadets must necessarily undergo are quite sufficient to cure them of any undue egotism with which they may be afflicted upon entering the Academy. The spirit which dictates hazing and its official counterpart, a harsh instead of a mild mode of imparting military instructions and enforcing obedience, is radically wrong.

Perhaps even more important than his denunciation were Schofield's clear guidelines of alternative, positive behavior:

> The best and most successful commanders of all grades are those who win the respect, confidence and affection of their subordinates by justice and firmness, tempered by kindness. The discipline which makes the soldiers of a free country reliable in battle is not to be gained by harsh or tyrannical treatment. On the contrary, such treatment is far more likely to destroy than to make an Army.

Unfortunately, the Booz scandal twenty years later is an indication of the inefficacy of Schofield's efforts. Nine days after Booz resigned, a new Superintendent, Albert Mills, arrived, and sought vigorously to suppress the hazing of plebes. His efforts brought him into extraordinary conflict with cadets, resulting in "a lengthy series of confrontations which appeared at times to reach mutinous proportions," according to Dillard.

In the 1920s, Superintendent Douglas MacArthur echoed Schofield's sentiments. While he acknowledged the less desirable soldiers who had comprised some previous armies, MacArthur suggested that World War I had "involved the efforts of every man, woman and child in the countries affected." Therefore, soldiers were now of "a higher type," for whom "discipline no longer required extreme methods. Men generally needed only to be told what to do, rather than be forced by the fear of consequence of failure."

MacArthur and his predecessor as Superintendent, General Samuel Tillman, codified written rules for the conduct of a "Fourth Class System." These rules left less doubt as to what forms of behavior were officially condoned. Nonetheless, the power of institutional rules was not equal to the power that fueled cadets' traditional behavior, and the abuses continued, their volume waxing and waning over the years.

Dwight D. Eisenhower returned from World War II with a concern similar to that of MacArthur after World War I. In 1946, he wrote to the Superintendent at West Point, Maxwell Taylor, suggesting that instruction should be undertaken at the Academy to "awaken the majority of cadets to the necessity for handling human problems on a human basis. . . ."

Still, by the mid-twentieth century, Schofield's ardent speech had been reduced to a mere bit of prose for plebes to memorize and be forced to recite upon demand by upperclass cadets. While the speech was surely inspiring to plebes, and its sentiments of positive benefit, the awkward fact is that plebes were often required to recite "Schofield's Definition of

Discipline" *at the very moment they were being hazed by upper-classmen.*

The explanation of the failures to reform the plebe system is complicated and multifaceted. For one thing, no matter how diligently opposed, the West Point administration lacked the wherewithal to control the behavior of upperclass cadets when officers were not watching them.

Furthermore, the highest motivation among the cadets for hazing was a conviction among upperclass ex-plebes that, despite the hardships endured, hazing had been good for them. And indeed, apart from gross abuses, it *had* been good for them; cadets reaching the end of plebe year felt extremely proud of surviving a trial by fire, of "running a gauntlet" which put "iron in their souls." Year after year, plebes themselves recounted to boards of review the virtues of the system. The positive results convinced each plebe that the experience had been beneficial to them and would be good for their successors.

Indeed, the fact that significant profit came to plebes from the plebe system even gave pause to those who had the strongest misgivings about it—so much pause that, perhaps, some of the efforts at reform were no better than halfhearted. Their misgivings, on the other hand, are best understood by taking the perspective not of the plebes, but rather of the upperclass cadets who purveyed the plebe system—and considering its effects on them as developing leaders.

Returning from World War I, Douglas MacArthur, according to historian Roger Nye, was disturbed by "a picture of officers needlessly bullying their men, and he saw the seeds of this in the treatment of West Point plebes by their upperclassmen." Schofield, then MacArthur, then Eisenhower, all expressed doubts about the harsh, negative leadership style of many American officers.

The leadership style of officers who had graduated from West Point often bore a strong resemblance to the behavior of upperclass cadets toward plebes; that dysfunctional style of leadership had followed them outside of the Academy. *Though the plebes may have benefited from the plebe system, the upper classes suffered.* In light of this dilemma, the pressure for reform of the system continued unabated. Given the repeated failures of previous attempts at reform, by the 1980s, the odds of success of any future reform were quite low.

Despite the long odds against success, Lieutenant General Dave R. Palmer, by then Superintendent at West Point, again undertook reform. Palmer had wisely learned a lesson from the history of the plebe system. Before attempting any specific changes, he established over several years a receptive *context* for reform. Under his lead, the Academy articulated publicly for the first time its long-standing commitment to developing leaders as its fundamental purpose.

With the purpose of developing leaders as its guide, the Academy faculty explored every aspect of the cadets' four-year experience. Each element was scrutinized and, in some cases, altered, to ensure that it contributed to a coherent framework for leadership development. Examined thusly, the shortcomings of the "Fourth Class System" became more and more apparent and were reported in findings of two different review committees.

The stage was set for change. The Academy's "dimensions of leadership" had been developed and became the basis for cadets' evaluations of subordinate cadets. The Academy's "principles of leader-subordinate relationships" had been drafted, reviewed, approved, published, and adopted as a guide for all personnel at West Point, from the top of the hierarchy down. These principles established a positive explanation of the style of leadership expected of upperclass cadets. (Again, these "dimensions" and "principles" are quoted at the end of this chapter.)

Due to continued emphasis on the Academy's leadership goals, the upperclass cadets began to experience a transformation in self-image. For the first time in West Point's history they began to think of themselves more as developing leaders than as purveyors of a harsh but necessary plebe system.

With these preparations in place, the Superintendent took his final step, arranging for three separate constituencies —the cadets, the alumni, and the faculty—to study for a year the possibility of changing the plebe system.

While the three groups disagreed about the extent of changes that were necessary, all fully agreed that the "Fourth Class System" should be replaced by a "four-class system." With a "four-class system," cadet life was no longer divided so reductively into the "us" and "them" separation of plebes and everyone else. The Academy adopted a new system which formalized the equal emphasis given to the development of leadership in all four classes.

During the initial years of implementation of the "four-class system," some upperclass cadets bemoaned the loss of some traditions of the earlier "Fourth Class System." Nonetheless, nearly all of them grudgingly admitted that the alternative made better sense. *They realized that they were leaders, and leaders don't treat their subordinates the way that cadets used to treat plebes.*

What set this attempt at reform apart from previous efforts was that the Superintendent recognized and accepted the power of the cadets to do what they chose when officers were not watching. *Instead of trying, as his predecessors had done, to force cadets to obey rules they did not believe in, he instead led them to believe in new rules.* The Academy invited the cadets to join in the pursuit of the institution's goal for them—that they become good leaders. Hence, the cadets themselves became empowered to effect the changes needed in their own behavior. They accepted the responsibility of that power, and changed themselves.

The benefits of the reform at West Point are seen throughout plebe year. Behavior which a few years ago was considered "cool" among upperclass cadets—harassing plebes in myriad, imaginative ways—is now "uncool." Now that upperclass cadets positively reinforce correct leadership behavior among themselves, peer pressure is working in favor of positive leadership.

To the surprise of some observers, the plebes now learn more quickly than before. For instance, one veteran tactical officer was amazed to report that on a recent R-day, his plebes were almost "in step" as they marched off the Plain after the swearing-in ceremony—an indication of how much they had learned about marching on their first day. In an earlier era, on R-day plebes were so distracted by the harassment of their "leaders" that their concentration on the skills to be learned was severely inhibited.

Furthermore, the Academy has for many years conducted interviews with plebes who choose to resign and go elsewhere. In past years, many complained as they departed about the style and quality of leadership they experienced at the hands of upperclass cadets. In recent years, such complaints from resignees during Beast Barracks dropped from a rate of forty per summer to only two or three.

West Point is a much stronger leadership institution now that it follows its own advice. But it came to this realization S-L-O-W-L-Y.

FRAMEWORKS FOR UNDERSTANDING LEADERSHIP

PRINCIPLES OF LEADER-SUBORDINATE RELATIONSHIPS

a. Leaders make clear to subordinates, early in the relationship, their commitment to the highest values of the military profession. Leaders abide by those values and encourage subordinates to do the same.

b. Leaders make clear their expectations of subordinates, knowing that demanding but achievable standards are expressions of confidence in subordinates. Leaders assist subordinates in learning how to meet those expectations, provide feedback to subordinates on performance and, finally, hold subordinates responsible to perform.

c. Leaders seek to foster within subordinates a motivation to do the job well, based on the subordinates' respect for and trust of their leaders. Leaders seek to earn that trust by consistent, respectful treatment of others and by adherence to high standards of personal conduct.

d. Leaders attempt to satisfy subordinates' needs so that the subordinate can contribute productively to the accomplishment of the mission.

e. Leaders take the initiative in fostering open, two-way communication.

f. Leaders provide the subordinates the rationale for tasks —thus building a foundation of trust on which to require performance without such rationale should this become necessary.

g. Leaders promote self-esteem in subordinates by providing positive feedback, by enabling subordinates to experience success, by building on subordinates' strengths, by avoiding situations in which subordinates cannot succeed, by refusing to demean subordinates, and by assisting subordinates in setting realistic, meaningful goals.

h. Leaders seek more from subordinates than mere compliance, drawing out when appropriate their knowledge, initiative, skills, understanding, and judgment to advance mission accomplishment.

i. Leaders do not seek to gain privilege or comfort at the expense of subordinates and suffer hardship along with subordinates when called upon to do so.

j. Leaders accept mistakes, affording subordinates opportunities to learn through experience; subordinates, in turn, strive to learn the lessons well.

k. Leaders praise in public and admonish in private.

l. Leaders punish when necessary, while insuring that the punishment is swift; is suited in kind and amount to the subordinate's failure; is directed at the behavior, not the person; and is designed to help the subordinate avoid the behavior in the future.

m. Both leaders and subordinates respect one another's value and personal dignity and manifest that respect in their actions.

n. Subordinates work for the success of the leader's decisions (assuming they are legal and ethical), providing honest advice before a decision is reached and working wholeheartedly to support it afterward.

o. Subordinates do not withhold cooperation from leaders who sometimes fail to practice the above principles.

LEADERSHIP DIMENSIONS

a. *Duty Motivation*. Commitment to doing what ought to be done (regarding stated and implied missions and tasks) based on the expectations of one's assigned duty position; commitment to placing requirements of the mission before personal interests; actions that indicate persistence in the attempt to achieve high standards of performance from oneself, subordinates, and others.

b. *Military Bearing*. Maintaining Army standards of military appearance, manner, and courtesy.

c. *Teamwork*. Those actions that indicate commitment to achievement of group or organizational goals: timely and effective discharge of operational and organizational duties and obligations; working effectively with others; compliance with and active support of organizational goals and policies.

d. *Influencing Others*. The art of using appropriate interpersonal styles and methods in guiding individuals (subordinates, peers, superiors) or groups toward task accomplishment and/or resolution of conflicts/disagreements; actively attempting to affect events to achieve goals.

e. *Consideration of Others.* Those actions that indicate a sensitivity to and regard for the feelings and needs of others and an awareness of the impact of one's own behavior on them; being supportive of and fair with others (subordinates, peers, and superiors).

f. *Planning and Organization.* The ability to establish a course of action for oneself and others to accomplish specific goals; establishing priorities and planning appropriate allocation of time and resources and/or proper assignment of personnel.

g. *Delegating.* The ability and inclination to use the talents of subordinates effectively; the allocation of decision-making and other authority to the appropriate subordinates.

h. *Supervising.* The ability to establish procedures for monitoring and regulating processes, tasks, or activities of subordinates and one's own job activities and responsibilities; taking action to monitor the results of delegated assignments or projects.

i. *Developing Subordinates.* The art of developing the competence and self-confidence of subordinates through role modeling and/or training and development activities related to their current or future duties.

j. *Decision-Making.* The ability to reach sound, logical conclusions based on analysis of factual information and the readiness to take action based on those conclusions.

k. *Oral and Written Communication.* The ability to express oneself effectively in individual or group situations, orally or in writing; includes utilizing good grammatical form, gestures, and other non-verbal communications.

l. *Professional Ethics.* Maintaining ethical, moral, and Army professional standards and values; accepting and acknowledging full responsibility for one's own actions.

13

The End of Leadership Is to
Stand for Something Good

The three greatest challenges of my life were entering West Point, entering the Army, and after twenty-seven years, re-entering civilian life. This surprises some people, who assume that the most challenging experience in a soldier's life is combat.

Of course, I do not want to minimize either the horrific or the heart-wrenching aspects of war. But because I experienced them within the familiar context of an organization to which I belonged and had acclimatized myself, the nature of the stress they placed on me was quite different from those three instances of profound transition when I had to move from familiar environments to completely strange ones. Those changes represented radical alterings of my entire life —much of my previous knowledge, the habits I'd acquired, almost everything that had been "me" had to be reinvented.

However, each transition was easier than the last. The

comparative facility of my latest progression is, of course, in part, because I am older, more experienced, and hence, more capable and confident. Looking back, though, I see how thoroughly my preparation at West Point readied me for the Army, and indeed civilian life.

The lessons I learned there, outlined in this book, continue to serve me. At this point, when I have to make difficult decisions, the principle of the harder right is deeply ingrained. When I am trying to train my subordinates to be both obedient and independent, I consider the early lessons I learned at the Academy. My experiences in teamwork at Camp Buckner were the beginning of teamwork strategies I employ today. Similarly, I hope that this book can provide the same kind of instructive suggestions for you.

DIRECTING THE ORGANIZATION FROM A POSITION OF CHARACTER

There are many commendable features of West Point's leadership program. It's comprehensive. It employs a logical progression. It is both pragmatic and theoretical. But I believe that what distinguishes West Point's leadership training most of all is the *end* it pursues. The West Point way of leading stems from deeply rooted principles. The cadet who succeeds in the West Point way becomes a leader of *character*.

Leadership is inherently neither good nor evil. It can serve either end. Leaders of character use their abilities to serve the public good, as best as they can discern it.

Leaders should not be afraid to direct their organizations

to stand for something good. If they do, the members of the organizations are dignified, and elevated above their own self-interest to a higher purpose outside themselves, one which is worthy of their commitment. This gives meaning to their individual lives, and energy to their collective purpose.

CARING FOR PEOPLE

Leaders of character value the people whom they lead and serve, in contrast to leaders without character, who abuse people as a means toward self-serving ends. Leaders who value people are motivated by a desire to serve the *ends* of people, fostering the improvement of their individual lives and the advancement of society as a whole, by means that respect the dignity of those people who are embarked on the journey together with their leaders.

As sternly self-disciplined as any West Pointer has ever been, Robert E. Lee's affection for his subordinates was nevertheless obvious to them. This is accented by a story told about his actions during the Wilderness Campaign, a bloody and bitter phase of the Civil War.

It was May 6, 1864, the second day of the campaign's fierce fighting. Mounted on his horse Traveler, Lee rode along the lines of weary soldiers just prior to their entry into battle. He was told by their commander, "General, these men are the brave Virginians." He gazed in silence at the soldiers, painfully aware that many of the men before him would lose their lives that day.

He uttered not a word. He removed his hat and passed slowly, bareheaded, down the line. Tears filled his eyes. Finally, he turned and silently rode away. Minutes later, as the men moved forward to charge, one tall youth, his voice choked with emotion, ran forward and shouted, "Any man who won't fight after what the general just said is a *&%!@# coward!" Another soldier, who survived the battle, recalled Lee's comportment and declared, "It was the most eloquent address ever delivered."

Lee struggled as a leader to find ways to both protect the lives of his followers and still achieve their collective goals. When he could not, it hurt in the depths of his soul, and his soldiers could see the hurt written on his face. Because leaders of character *care deeply* about both the mission and the people who must accomplish it, they are liable to experience great internal conflict and deep anguish.

A LEGACY OF EXCELLENCE

At the conclusion of the West Point graduation ceremony, cadets traditionally throw their hats high into the air, and most of them are scooped up by the children of the families in attendance. One recent graduate told me that as a child he had attended a West Point graduation, and collected a hat, which he cherished through the years, occasionally wondering to whom it had belonged and what had become of him. As a result, when it came his turn to throw his own hat, he included in its brim several personal mementos, as well as a letter describing himself and the values which had attracted him to the Academy. He was passing on to another youngster the inspiration which he had received.

Similarly, Joe Dudley, a highly successful businessman in

North Carolina, passes on to future leaders the help he once received. He grew up in a large, poor family in a small, rural town. Inspired by his parents' insistence on the importance of education, Dudley worked his way through college selling Fuller brushes from a mail-order sales kit for which he had paid ten dollars. He later headed Fuller Brush, and then started his own company supplying beauty products designed for the needs of African-Americans. Now, Dudley passes on his success and good fortune by sponsoring fifty young men and women each year. By providing financial assistance and personal mentoring in skills needed to succeed as leaders, Dudley is inspiring these young people just as he had been inspired by his parents.

LEADERSHIP AS A WAY OF LIFE

I am sure that my leadership education has made me a more effective leader, and a more effective person. A very important principle that I learned at the Academy is that developing as a leader is a lifelong commitment. It's an evolving process. Four years at West Point cannot teach you all you need to know any more than a two-year MBA program can. But they have provided me, and thousands of others, with the basis for a lifetime of growth.

Throughout my career in the service, I heard it said wryly many times that the biggest demotion in the Army is from senior cadet at West Point to second lieutenant in the Army. The remark is spoken "half-jokingly." It's half-true, because fourth-year cadets are the senior members of West Point's hierarchy. After being "kings of the hill" for a year, and then celebrated by the pomp and circumstance of their various graduation ceremonies, it's hard not to feel let down when they enter the service and become the low man on the totem pole of the Officers' Corps. They must begin again.

Yet that passage mirrors many passages in life. Each time we get a promotion, change jobs, or apply our leadership expertise to a new venue, it's a new beginning.

If the remark is half-true, it's also half-false. Like all leaders who bring their previous experience to new leadership challenges, West Pointers who enter the Army are beginning again—but they are beginning *exponentially*. They may be the lowest rung of officer, but they are immediately entrusted with leading the ranks of all enlisted soldiers. Furthermore, they are being launched on what, for the majority, will be long and productive careers in the Army, with all of the knowledge and experience they have garnered at West Point —the benefit of the wisdom the Academy has acquired in its nearly two-hundred-year existence.

I think of West Point as a four-year preamble to a forty-year career. In quick increments over four short years, cadets are introduced to the four levels of leadership that they are likely to reencounter at a much slower pace, in the course of their professional lives. As they progress, the Academy will continue to provide them a handy point of reference.

West Point offers far more than a kit bag of tools and techniques for the leader. Rather, by fostering leadership rooted in character, it offers the prospect of lives filled with a sense of purpose and the deep joy such a life brings. It is my hope that through this book, West Point can make the same offer to you.

BRAVE WORDS
FOR LEADERS
IN TOUGH
SITUATIONS

I am a great believer in the capacity of the written and spoken word to inspire and motivate, especially in times of trouble. Admiral James Stockdale was a student both of the Bible story of Job and the Stoic philosopher Epictetus. When he was shot down over North Vietnam, as he drifted to earth in his parachute, to the certainty of becoming a prisoner of war, he thought, "Epictetus, here I come." He knew that the words he'd studied would soon become the very words that would keep him alive through the ordeal he was approaching. He was about to make his life in Epictetus' company, which as a POW for seven years, is exactly what he did.

At West Point, leaders learn that words are to be taken as seriously as actions. The words of others that have inspired me, often to perform beyond my ability, are words I include here. I hope they inspire you as well.

ON WEST POINT

"The purpose of the United States Military Academy is to provide the nation with leaders of character who serve the common defense." —West Point's statement of purpose

"Your duty here at West Point has been to fit men to do well in wars. But it is a noteworthy fact that you have also fitted them to do well in peace." —Theodore Roosevelt

"No group of men has participated more fully than West Pointers in the century and a half that saw this raw continent transformed into the most powerful country of the world." —Thomas J. Fleming in *West Point: The Men and Times of the United States Military Academy*

"It was still the West Point of Grant, Sherman, Sheridan, Schofield and Howard. The deep impression these great men made during their visits to West Point in our day went far to inspire us with the soldier's spirit of self-sacrifice, duty and honor." —General John J. Pershing

ON THE MEANING OF WEST POINT'S MOTTO—''DUTY, HONOR, COUNTRY''

"They build your basic character, they mold you for your future roles as the custodians of the nation's defense, they make you strong enough to know when you are weak, and brave enough to face yourself when you are afraid. They teach you to be proud and unbending in honest failure, but humble and gentle in success; not to substitute words for actions, nor to seek the path of comfort, but to face the stress and spur of difficulty and challenge; to learn to stand up in the storm but to have compassion on those who fall; to master yourself before you seek to master others; to have a heart that is clean, a goal that is high; to learn to laugh yet never forget how to weep; to reach into the future yet never neglect the past; to be serious yet never to take yourself too seriously; to be modest so that you will remember the simplicity of true greatness, the open mind of true wisdom; the meekness of true strength. They give you a temper of the will, a quality of the imagination, a vigor of the emotions, a freshness of the deep springs of life, a temperamental predominance of courage over timidity, an appetite for adventure over love of ease. They create in your heart the sense of wonder, the unfailing hope of what next, and the joy and inspiration of life. They teach you in this way to be an officer and a gentleman.

"You are the leaven which binds together the entire fabric of our national system of defense. From your ranks come the great captains who hold the nation's destiny in their hands the moment the war tocsin sounds. The Long Gray Line has never failed us. Were you to do so, a million ghosts in olive drab, in brown khaki, in blue and gray, would rise from their white crosses thundering those magic words—Duty, Honor, Country.

"This does not mean that you are war mongers. On the contrary, the soldier, above all other people, prays for peace, for he must suffer and bear the deepest wounds and scars of war. But always in our ears ring the ominous words of Plato, that wisest of all philosophers: 'Only the dead have seen the end of war.' " —Douglas MacArthur, addressing cadets in May 1962

ON LEADERS

"Tactically aggressive (loves a fight), strength of character, steadiness of purpose, acceptance of responsibility, energy, and good health and strength." —George Patton's notion of the six necessary qualities of a good general, scribbled in the margin of his copy of Fieberger's *Elements of Strategy* when he was a West Point cadet

"Being on the teaching staff [at West Point] had not only sharpened my wits, it had broadened and matured me considerably. In these years, I began to read seriously and study military history and biography, learning a great deal from the mistakes of my predecessors." —General Omar Bradley

"The best and most successful commanders . . . are those who win the respect, confidence and affection of their subordinates by justice and firmness, tempered by kindness. The discipline which makes the soldiers of a free country reliable in battle is not to be gained by harsh or tyrannical treatment. On the contrary, such treatment is far more likely to destroy than to make an Army." —General John Schofield, both a West Point Superintendent and graduate

ON REGARD FOR OTHERS

"It is possible to impart instruction and to give commands in such manner and such a tone of voice to inspire in the soldier no feeling but an intense desire to obey." —John Schofield

"He who feels the respect which is due to others cannot fail to inspire in them regard for himself, while he who feels, and hence manifests, disrespect toward others, especially his inferiors, cannot fail to inspire hatred against himself." —John Schofield

"A leader should possess human understanding and consideration for others. Men are not robots and should not be treated as such. I do not by any means suggest coddling. But men are intelligent, complicated beings who will respond favorably to human understanding and consideration. By these means their leader will get maximum effort from each of them. He will also get loyalty." —Omar Bradley

ON CARING

"Affection shall solve the problems of freedom yet!" —Walt Whitman, upon hearing of the compassionate terms of surrender offered to Robert E. Lee by Ulysses S. Grant, both West Pointers, at the Appomattox Court House

• • •

"The leader must have time to listen to his men. It is easy to look important and say, 'I haven't got time,' but each time the leader does it, he drives one more nail in the coffin of the team spirit whose life he should really be cherishing." —Lincoln Andrews, a West Point faculty member under MacArthur

"Perhaps the most important of the fundamentals for the military leader to realize is the deep-seated desire of every individual to maintain his self-respect and to have his right to self-respect recognized by those around him." —Lincoln Andrews

"Build on what a man is—don't tear him down." —General Creighton Abrams, a West Point graduate, four-star commander of all U.S. forces in Vietnam, and Army Chief of Staff

ON SINCERITY

". . . above all a leader must be genuine—his own true self, not an imitation of some other, be that other ever so successful." —Lincoln Andrews

ON SELF-COMMAND

"If anyone is unhappy, he is so for himself alone." —Epictetus, *The Enchiridion*

·   ·   ·

"Reason will never tell you to be dejected and broken-hearted." —Epictetus

ON INTEGRITY

"No great soldier ever rose to eminence as a military commander who was not primarily a man of character. It is for this reason that West Point takes the development of character as a formal objective to be pursued by all available means." —General Maxwell Taylor

"West Point taught us not the skill to unravel conflicting political creeds . . . but rather to illustrate by our lives manly courage and loyalty to our convictions." —Edward Porter Alexander, Lee's chief of artillery

ON TENACITY

"I need men who will stay on the job until I get tired of having them there or until I say they may abandon it. I shall turn it over to the Army." —Theodore Roosevelt upon appointing George Washington Goethals, West Point class of 1880, to take over the Panama Canal project, abandoned by two civilian predecessors

DOUGLAS MACARTHUR'S
PRINCIPLES OF LEADERSHIP

Do I heckle my subordinates or strengthen and encourage them?

Do I use moral courage in getting rid of subordinates who have proven themselves beyond doubt to be unfit?

Have I done all in my power by encouragement, incentive and spur to salvage the weak and erring?

Do I know by NAME and CHARACTER a maximum number of subordinates for whom I am responsible? Do I know them intimately?

Am I thoroughly familiar with the technique, necessities, objectives and administration of my job?

Do I lose my temper at individuals?

Do I act in such a way as to make my subordinates WANT to follow me?

Do I delegate tasks which should be mine?

Do I arrogate everything to myself and delegate nothing?

Do I develop my subordinates by placing on each one as much responsibility as he can stand?

Am I interested in the personal welfare of each of my subordinates, as if he were a member of my family?

Have I the calmness of voice and manner to inspire confidence, or am I inclined to irascibility and excitability?

Am I a constant example to my subordinates in character, dress, deportment and courtesy?

Am I inclined to be nice to my superiors and mean to my subordinates?

Is my door open to my subordinates?

Do I think more of POSITION than JOB?

Do I correct a subordinate in front of others?

Acknowledgments

In late 1989, Ms. Harriet Rubin, an editor for Doubleday, suggested by letter to then-Superintendent of the United States Military Academy, Lieutenant General Dave Palmer, that the West Point way of leadership should be made more widely known. Both he and I agreed with her suggestion and, with his steady encouragement, I responded to the need.

During the years in which the book was in preparation, I enjoyed the enormously helpful wisdom of several friends on the faculty and staff at the Academy who were willing to read part or all of multiple preliminary drafts. They included Dave Palmer, Howard Graves, Barney Forsyth, Bruce Bell, Steve Hammond, Howard Prince, John and Bill Wattendorf, Tony Hartle, and Jim Golden. In addition, two friends and fellow West Pointers, Walt Ulmer and Jack Wheeler, read and commented generously on an early draft.

During the final stages of composition, I was greatly assisted by a team suggested by and including Harriet Rubin and another editor, Janet Coleman. It was Harriet who con-

Acknowledgments

ceived the book and believed there was a story to be told. Both she and Janet brought wonderfully polished editorial skill to my drafts, and Janet particularly devoted herself above and beyond the call of duty to coordinating our team effort and reworking and finalizing my material. In addition the team included two others: first, a highly talented young writer, David Lida, who assisted me through interviews in bringing more of my personal experiences into the account and who brought his own literary gifts to the task of rewrites of my early drafts; second, a fellow West Pointer who graduated more recently than I, Chris Frawley, who spent many hours with me and the other members in conference calls helping to jog my memory of cadet days and what it felt like to experience West Point. It is this team which deserves the credit for bringing the book into its final form.

CURRENCY

DOUBLEDAY